SELLING

THE

FAMILY
SILVER

SELLING THE FAMILY SILVER

HAS PRIVATIZATION WORKED?

COLIN CHAPMAN

Hutchinson
Business
Books

First published in Great Britain in 1990 by
Hutchinson Business Books Limited
And imprint of Random Century Limited
20 Vauxhall Bridge Road, London SW1V 2SA

Random Century Australia (Pty) Limited
20 Alfred Street, Milsons Point, Sydney
New South Wales 2061, Australia

Random Century New Zealand Limited
9–11 Rothwell Avenue, Albany, Glenfield
Auckland 10, New Zealand

Century Hutchinson South Africa (Pty) Limited
PO Box 337, Bergvlei 2012, South Africa

Set in Plantin by CentraCet, Cambridge

Printed and bound in Great Britain by
Mackays of Chatham PLC, Chatham, Kent

British Library Cataloguing in Publication Data

Chapman, Colin
Selling the family silver: has privatization worked?
1. Great Britain. Public sector. Privatization
I. Title
354.4107'2

ISBN 0-09-174241-2

Contents

CONTENTS

Acknowledgements

MOST OF THE people who have helped me gather information and background for this book prefer – even insist – on remaining anonymous. Many of the true stories about privatization are not to be found in the news bulletins, where, regrettably, the emphasis has been more towards hype than hard fact. And many of those whose bank balances have been enriched by the great privatization process in train throughout Mrs Margaret Thatcher's first decade in office have been reluctant to detail their roles. Such is the fear of the Official Secrets Act, originally designed to protect our defences, but now used to spare official embarrassment.

For matters of record, I am grateful to a number of Government departments, and to the excellent information services of the *Financial Times* and the London Business School. The chairman, members and staff of the International Stock Exchange in London have been extremely supportive and helpful. Susan Wheeler has given me generous assistance, and professor Peter Drucker's book, *The Age of Discontinuity*, provides the most rational explanation for privatization. I also must thank my wife, Susan Grice, for reading the manuscript, and for undertaking many of the tasks I should have done had I not been writing this book.

Introduction

PRIVATIZATION IS ABOUT ownership. If we own a piece of land, or a home placed on it, we can be clear about title. It is ours to enjoy and, subject to any outstanding mortgage, we are free to sell the title to whom we wish.

Businesses that belong to the state are different. In theory they are ours. In many cases, such as the railways or Britain's post-War steelworks, they were bought for our benefit by left-of-centre politicians, who used our money, through taxation, to appropriate them from their private owners. The politicians then ran these businesses as if they belonged, not to us, but to them. They created funds, known as 'gilts', in order to be able to run them mostly at a loss. In Britain, for much of the recent past, these bonds were in a rapidly devaluing currency. These days they would be called 'junk bonds'. Most of us lost money, in real terms, by lending our money to the Government, especially if we did so via the Post Office. We also, through further taxation, paid for the interest the Government credited to us.

Another set of politicians moved in. They decided they should hand back to us the businesses we were already supposed to own. But instead of *giving* them back to us, they made us pay for them. This meant spending tens of millions of pounds in fees on intermediaries in the City of London, which helped them through a sticky patch but cost us dear. When we had spent our savings to buy these businesses back from ourselves, the Government then decided to give some of us some of this money back through tax cuts, so that we would re-elect them to carry out more of the same.

If there is a winner in all this, it is not the public. But at least there is a chance that British Telecom, British Gas and other great concerns may now be run more efficiently than by the politicians. But it is only a chance. Politicians love to interfere.

· 1 ·
Communism fails: privatization begins

'Privat: Middle English proverb from Latin, privatus, not belonging to the State, not in public life, deprived of office, from the past participle of privare, to deprive, release'
– American Heritage Dictionary

'Greed is good'
– Gordon Gekko, insider trader in the Hollywood film, *Wall Street*

WHEN HISTORIANS COME to write their definitive analysis of the second half of the twentieth century, two trends will be paramount.

The first will be that many Western leaders – and not a few businesspeople, public servants, writers and intellectuals – spent much of the first four decades worrying about a philosophy called Communism, which in the late 50s threatened to become fairly pervasive. The United States went to war over it in Vietnam, and lost. One of the many arguments in favour of the Vietnam War was the 'Domino Theory': that, unless South Vietnam and Cambodia were kept free from the taint of Communism, the other countries of South-East Asia would fall, like dominos. They didn't, but Communism's own dominos in

Eastern Europe collapsed, one by one, choosing a social market economy instead of the straitjacket of Marxist-Leninism.

The second trend, running parallel with the first, will be privatization. One by one governments have been divesting themselves of great state-owned corporations. Britain has led the world in ridding the taxpayer of the burden and the public servant of the responsibility for huge businesses like telecommunications, gas supply, water and electricity.

But in Britain, as elsewhere, the popularity of privatization is relatively recent. Indeed, the second half of the twentieth century began with the British Government determined to increase rather than reduce public ownership. Throughout the 50s the cry of the Labour Party was to take over the 'commanding heights of the economy' so that private entrepreneurs could not make excessive profits at the expense of the people. This cry was not only adopted in much of Europe, but it formed the foundation of almost every post-colonial Third World economy, with disastrous consequences.

Yet only five years after British investors queued in the streets to lodge their applications for shares in British Telecom and British Gas, the Poles were forming their own lines to buy more than 20 million $2 shares in the Universal distribution group. Now privatization is in full swing in countries where, only a few years ago, the concept was inconceivable. The most symbolic change of all is taking place in Gdansk on the Baltic in Poland. Even the Lenin shipyard, named after one of the founding fathers of Communism, and the cradle of the revolt against totalitarianism led by Lech Walesa and the trade union Solidarity, is up for sale.

Ironically, as the century draws to a close, the British, the Belgians and the French are back in Africa and Asia, not as colonialists, but as highly-paid professional advisers, invited to produce reports on how privatization, including transnational ownership of state enterprises, can revitalize depressed and bankrupt economies.

Whether the need to use privatization to lift a stagnant and moribund British economy was the real reason for the introduction of this policy on a large scale in the years of Mrs Margaret

Thatcher's government is very questionable. Initially, it was unpopular with many Tories, including several previous Prime Ministers. One of them, Harold Macmillan, referred to it as akin to 'selling the family silver'.

The official reason given was that privatization would increase competition between industries, thereby providing better and more efficient services, in contrast with state monopolies, seen by Conservative Party ministers as uncompetitive and bureaucratic. This is highly questionable. The truth of the matter is that there are many reasons why privatization was introduced, but the Government keeps changing their order of priority to suit the mood at the time. Another reason was that privatized industry would attract more investment. A third was that the proceeds of privatization could be used to reduce the public sector borrowing requirement.

As the accountancy group Price Waterhouse stated in a booklet, *Privatization: Learning the lessons from the UK experience*:

> There was certainly no long-term master plan at the outset . . . it evolved, haphazardly, picking off what seemed to be easy targets in the early stages as politicians and civil servants felt their way towards the most effective techniques.

Another commentator, Paul Batchelor, head of the privatization unit at the accountancy firm Coopers and Lybrand, said:

> One of the interesting things is how the political rationale has changed. The Government has very subtly moved its rationale. Privatization hardly featured in the Tory thinking before 1980. It wasn't even mentioned in the manifesto of 1979.

At first, ministers stressed increased efficiency and the fact that a smaller public sector would allow them to reduce taxes, which they, of course, did. Indeed, but for the sums of money released to the Exchequer by the sales of British Telecom and British Gas, the very large tax cuts enjoyed by the public in the late 80s would not have materialized. Critics have argued that the money realized by the asset sales should have been used for other purposes: for instance, improving social services such as education and health. The choice, however, was not that simple. If taxes had remained high, there would have been little incentive to hold shares.

As the 80s wore on, the Conservatives perceived, partly to their surprise, that popular capitalism could, in fact, be popular. As we shall see, that proved to be an optimistic view. But by 1989, the number of people owning shares had trebled to six million. And more than 1.2 million council house tenants had purchased their own properties. By the time the decade of the 90s began, one in four owned shares, compared with one in 14 before privatization.

It has to be noted that few people have lost money from an investment in privatization. The securities house County Natwest WoodMackenzie analysed the post-privatization performance of a number of companies, including British Aerospace, Cable and Wireless, AB Ports, British Telecom, British Gas, British Airways, Rolls-Royce and the British Airports Authority, and found that only Rolls-Royce failed to outperform the market by a significant amount in the first half-year.

British Telecom, for instance, outperformed the market by 22 per cent, while British Gas did better by 10.5 per cent. For some inexplicable reason, the brokers left British Petroleum out of the package. BP shares fell 29 per cent below the issue price of £3.30, and more than two years later still had not topped it. But there were special reasons for that, as we shall see later.

Another way of looking at it has been provided by the Hoare Govett Privatization Index, which comprised all the companies floated on the market as part of the Thatcher privatization programme. In 1988, just prior to the water issue, the index was capitalized at £35 billion, which represented about 9 per cent of the market as a whole. Although privatization stocks were deeply affected by the global market crash of 1987, with British

Aerospace, Jaguar and Rolls-Royce being especially hard hit, the index bounded back and continued to outperform the FT All Share Index until Security Pacific, Hoare Govett's American owners, decided to cut back on research and discontinue it in 1989.

But British investors have long memories, and behave cautiously. Andrew Hugh Smith, chairman of London's International Stock Exchange, told a conference on wider share ownership in the Spring of 1990 how the turning point for individuals came with the onslaught on private wealth by the Wilson Labour government of 1964–70:

> From then on the pressures of penal taxation, disastrous economic management and rising rates of inflation, accompanied by increasing fiscal bias in favour of collective investment schemes, led to a progressive dimunition of private investor participation in our domestic equity market to the point where today less than 20 per cent of domestic equities are owned by private individuals.
>
> The markets are now dominated by institutional investors, by life insurance companies, by pension funds, and by collective investment schemes such as unit trusts. In London less than 100 fund management businesses effectively control institutional investment, and they in turn are serviced by a relatively small number of intermediaries, particularly in the field of research and investment advice.

RULE BRITANNIA

Britain has had the largest privatization programme. By the end of 1990, it will have raised almost £27 billion from asset sales.

Yet at one stage it looked as if this would be rivalled by the French. In France, in the mid-80s, the Gaullist government headed by Jacque Chirac had planned to dispose of over 200 billion French francs worth of state assets, in a sale of the century that would have dwarfed the Thatcher plans. Among the disposals on the Chirac list were the major state television network, TF1; 36 banks – including *les trois vieux*, the oldest in the country, Société Général, Banque National de Paris and Crédit Lyonnais; Renault, the state car maker; Gaz de France; and a host of other industrial concerns.

In the end, the Gaullists were defeated by the Socialists, led by Michel Rocard, who put a stop to privatization, but not before some of the banks and the industrial giant St Gobain had been taken into the private sector.

I think it unlikely that the disposal of the banks will make much difference in an economy as *dirigiste* as France's. Given Gallic pride, it is unthinkable that even conservatives would let major French financial institutions pass into foreign hands or be managed by those who could not be controlled in some other way by the Parisian Establishment.

Elsewhere in Europe, privatization has proceeded at a varying pace. In West Germany, for example, the Christian Democratic government led by Helmut Kohl decided to sell off completely its stake in two companies in which it had a major stake: Volkswagen, the car maker, and Veba, the energy and chemicals group. The sale of the Federal government's remaining one-fifth share in Volkswagen was no surprise, although VW is not completely clear of government control, since the state of Lower Saxony, led by 'Red' Oscar Lafontaine, still retains a minority holding. And it is thought that Gerhard Stoltenburg, the Finance Minister, will want the government to hold on to the 25 per cent stake in Veba until energy prices improve. It disposed of 75 per cent in 1984, and must now wish it had rid itself of its entire holding at that time. Together these two sales should raise the government DM 5.5 billion, on top of the DM 745 million expected to be collected from the disposal of 40 per cent of VIAG, an aluminium, energy and chemical group. Other plans in the pipeline in Germany include the part-privatization of energy group Prakia-Seismos and property and transport group Industrieverwaltungsgesellschaft, and the national airline Lufthansa, although the sale of the German airline was blocked by the fierce opposition of the Bavarians.

In South America, a major proponent of privatization is the Argentinian government, which wants to rid the state of no fewer than 350 companies over the next few years. These include the giant steel firm Somisa, and the petrochemical corporations Bahia Blanca, General Mosconi and Rio Tercero. But with its traditions of operating a corporate state, it is doubtful whether the government will be able to muster enough enthusiasm from investors for these sales.

Elsewhere, privatization is at an early stage. In Australia, the conservative opposition parties have adopted it as policy, but the policy has been accorded little media enthusiasm. Across the Tasman in New Zealand, the Labour government spent years bickering about it. An assortment of South-East Asian countries are considering selling off state assets – and some have hired British merchant bankers with experience of UK flotations to produce reports for them. In most cases it has been argued that financial markets need to be more flexible and open, with a greater public awareness of their role, before new policies are pushed through.

Privatization has also become one of the favoured policies of the World Bank and the International Monetary Fund, as they seek to deal with the problem of Third World debt. Soft loans are now as unfashionable as aid: the buzz word in Washington is now 'restructuring'. One form of reducing state spending and borrowing in this process of structural adjustment is to sell off state assets; many are assets in name only because they have become state liabilities. Privatization is one way a near-bankrupt nation can attract overseas capital.

The World Bank has assisted in about 30 privatization projects. Some of the smallest countries have been the most effective. In Africa, Togo has cut government ownership in 22 of its 72 state enterprises. Thailand has contracted private companies to run its passenger railways. Bangladesh is selling off shoe and textile mills. At the other end of the spectrum, Japan is privatizing telecommunications and railways.

Once upon a time one of the proudest symbols of nationhood was an airline. Even the smallest African country had to have one. Now airlines are being privatized by the dozen. All the shares in British Airways are now held in the private sector. Neither Britain nor the United States has a government carrier. In Europe, Lufthansa, KLM, Finnair and Air France have been partially sold to the private sector. In Asia, the airlines of Japan, Malaysia and Singapore have been totally or partially sold off. Air New Zealand has been privatized.

Little, it seems, can escape privatization. Gordon Gekko in the film *Wall Street*, convicted of insider trading, can look forward to several years of reflection in the air-conditioned condominium-like comfort of a private gaol. In the United States there are now nine privately-run prisons – in Florida, New Mexico, Texas and Tennessee. Prisoner costs have been cut by one-third.

But if the Conservative's purpose of privatization was to introduce popular capitalism – to turn the British into a nation of shareholders – then this objective has not been achieved, whatever politicians may say. For while it is true that one in four families now own shares, almost two-thirds of the 11.5 million shareholders have shares in only one company. It is likely the company will either be the one they work for, or British Telecom or British Gas. And although individuals have picked up small portfolios from privatization issues, they have been withdrawing their money from the stock markets as a whole. More than £3 billion in each of recent years have been withdrawn by private individuals from the stock markets. In 1957, two-thirds of the shares on registers in Britain were in private hands. By 1979, this had fallen to a third; by 1990, it was down to one-fifth.

So the British have certainly not developed a real taste for share ownership or share trading. This is not surprising, given the City of London's antipathy towards private investors from the middle or working classes. Many have traded in their shares for unit trust schemes, which may well prove to be a mistake. The major privatization stocks offer a sound defence against inflation and have outperformed the market. A personal equity plan using British Airways or British Telecom is likely to be more efficient than a unit trust, where management costs now often tend to outweigh the advantages of such schemes.

What would it take to get individuals back into the market? Back-of-the-envelope calculations suggest that if individuals are to increase their stake from 20 per cent to, say, 30 per cent over the next ten years, they would have to invest at least £9 billion. This is improbable, given the possibility of the election of a Labour government committed to higher taxation of those on above average incomes.

Yet higher share ownership is not totally out of the question. In 1988, individuals put £26.6 billion into fixed assets, bonds and stocks, and increased their deposits in banks and building societies by £38.2 billion. The British love building societies, and why not? The societies may have too many branches, but their managers do not drive Porsches or act like lager louts, and the income percentage return on bank and building society deposits looks attractive when compared with the yield on ordinary shares.

Barclays Bank is one of the major High Street institutions that has been trying to make it easier for members of the public to own shares. It has established Barclayshare, a low-cost dealing service with an extra facility whereby certificates may be lodged with the bank and a yearly statement of dividends is prepared by the bank for the taxman. Other banks have followed suit.

Yet none of the banks appear to have marketed actively their share broking services. Perhaps this is not surprising. The banks generate profits from lending money to customers and from providing financial services such as pensions, unit trust investments and other savings schemes. By comparison with the earnings generated from these activities, the commission on share dealing for individuals is little more than a fringe activity.

· 2 ·

Business as musician in the Government orchestra

'It's like selling the family silver'
– Harold Macmillan, speaking in the House of Commons

'Reprivatization is hardly a creed of "fat cat millionaires" when Black Power advocates seriously propose making education in the slums "competitive" by turning it over to private enterprise competing for the tax dollar on the basis of proven performance in teaching ghetto children'
– Peter Drucker, *The Age of Discontinuity*

MANY PEOPLE CREDIT Margaret Thatcher with introducing the unattractive word 'privatization' into our lives. But while her British Conservative government may have been responsible for the start of the populist privatization push, she cannot take the credit for establishing the word in the English vocabulary. As might be expected it was an Americanism, created by the management guru and author Professor Peter Drucker.

Nor was the idea conceived by Thatcher or Tory think-tanks such as the Bow Group or the Conservative Political Research Centre. It was first outlined in detail by the Viennese-born Drucker in a chapter entitled 'The Sickness of Government' in his book, *The Age of Discontinuity: Guidelines to Our Changing Society* (Heinemann, 1969).

The Drucker thesis, published in the late 60s, argued that

'government is big rather than strong; that it is fat and flabby rather than powerful; that it costs a great deal but does not achieve much', and that disenchantment with it 'cuts across national boundaries and ideological lines'.

Given that this was written when the international trend was to push for more government, more state intervention, and more of a public assault on transnational corporations and the power of big business, Drucker's statement was certainly prescient. But as he said:

> We expected miracles – and that always produces dis- illusionment. Government, it was widely believed (though only subconsciously), would produce a great many things for nothing. Cost was thought a function of who did something rather than of what was being attempted.
>
> There is little doubt, for instance, that the British in adopting the National Health Service believed that medical care would cost nothing. . . . Nurses, doctors, hospitals, drugs, and so on have to be paid for by somebody. But everybody expected this 'somebody' to be somebody else.

Many of those who advocated public ownership did not usually do so because they thought it a panacea, though for some, like the Labour peer-turned-commoner, Tony Benn, it was clearly that. The argument was simply: 'Private business and profits are bad – *ergo* government ownership must be good'.

The experience of public ownership revealed its manifest disadvantages, and proved that dogma could not produce solutions. From Bucharest to Brooklyn corruption and closet corporatism generated a new, privileged class enjoying benefits that many a despotic monarch would envy. It certainly did not produce power for the people, or any of the other aspirations of Marx or Lenin. Since Gorbachev's rise to power in the Soviet Union the Russian press is full of examples of excessive self-enrichment by those who occupied high positions in state corporations. As one writer bitterly complained in *Pravda* on 7 March 1988: 'No one imagined that Soviet "millionaires" would appear in our society which is building Communism . . . certain individuals have managed to amass huge fortunes, they live in luxury.'

By 1968, when the Soviet tanks were driving across Czechoslovakia to crush the first fruits of rebellion against Communist Party domination, New York liberals were urging that garbage collections should be turned over to free enterprise. Having public services run by politicians and bureaucrats was – and is – a recipe for conflict between vested and selfish interests.

In arguing the case for privatization, Drucker stressed that the purpose of government was to govern – to present fundamental choices and to make fundamental decisions – and that this role was incompatible with 'doing':

> Any attempt to combine governing with 'doing' on a large scale, paralyses the decision-making capacity. Any attempt to make decision-making organs actually 'do', also means very poor 'doing'. They are not focused on 'doing'. They are not equipped for it. They are not fundamentally concerned with it.
>
> There is good reason why soldiers, civil servants and hospital administrators look to business management for concepts, principles, and practices. For business, during the last thirty years, has had to face, on a much smaller scale, the problems which modern government now faces: the incompatibility between 'governing' and 'doing'. Business management learned that the two have to be separated, and that the top organ, the decision-maker, has to be detached from 'doing'. Otherwise he does not make decisions, and the 'doing' does not get done either.

Thus, argued Drucker in 1969, splitting the two roles made it possible for top management to concentrate on direction and making important decisions, sloughing off implementation to operating managements, each with their own mission and goals, and with their own sphere of action and autonomy. He went on:

> If this lesson were applied to governments, the other institutions of society would rightly become the 'doers'. . . .

Government would start out by asking the question: 'How do these institutions work and what can they do?' It would then ask: 'How can political and social objectives be formulated and organized in such a manner as to become opportunities for performance for these institutions?' It would also ask: 'And what opportunities for accomplishment of political objectives do the abilities and capacities of these institutions offer to government?'

Drucker saw business as only one, albeit an important, musician in a structure whereby government was the composer and conductor, but an orchestra played the score.

It is important to confine business – and every other institution – to its own task. Reprivatization will, therefore, entail using other non-government institutions – the hospital, for instance, or the university – for other, non-economic 'doing' tasks. The design of new non-governmental, autonomous institutions as agents of social performance under reprivatization may well become a central job for tomorrow's political architects . . . .
We do not face a 'withering away of the state'. On the contrary, we need a vigorous, strong, and very active government. But we do face a choice between big but impotent government and a government that is strong because it confines itself to decision and direction and leaves the 'doing' to others. We do not face 'a return to laissez faire' in which the economy is left alone. The economic sphere cannot and will not be considered to lie outside the public domain. But the choices for the economy – as well as for all the other sectors – are no longer either complete government indifference or complete governmental control.

Drucker's book, though published more than two decades ago, is worth reading because it sets out in detail his formula for privatization: the best I can provide is an imperfect summary.

It also establishes that although Margaret Thatcher has followed some of the principles he outlines, both she and other
apostles of privatization have discarded many others. The
British experience is much more focused on business as the chief
vehicle for implementation of the policy. The Conservatives
have sought to remove both central and local government from
enterprises which they control, but they have not yet tackled
institutions which exist for the public good but which are, at
least in theory, independent. These include the British Broadcasting Corporation, the British Council and a variety of trusts
which depend on government funding for survival. The universities have not featured at all. Had Drucker's theories been
followed then the British universities would have been sustained, nourished and strengthened, rather than emasculated.
Building independent institutions other than for profit has not
really been on the British agenda.

It was not long after the publication of *The Age of Discontinuity*
that the word 'privatization' made its first appearance in British
political literature. It turned up in a Conservative Central
Office pamphlet published in the Heath era in May 1970. It
was called *A New Style of Government*. The author, David Howell,
MP, made a convincing case for smaller government and the
removal of bureaucrats by 'transferring functions and activities
back to the public sector or running them down altogether':

The need now is not to 'spend more on housing', or 'do
more to help research', or 'give more help to exporters', or
'spend more on hospitals', or 'introduce a fairer tax
system'. . . . It is to reinvolve the private sector in the
achievement of a national goal of good homes for all; it is
to harness and reduce the torrents of public money being
poured into government research institutions; it is to create
a framework in which private enterprise services make the
welfare services for exporters which have grown up in
government departments redundant; it is to reorganize the
whole management structure, finance and control of hospital administration.

Peter Drucker uses the unusually ugly word 'privatization' for this process. This at least distinguishes it from denationalization, which means something rather different, but it is still hideously clumsy.

The Heath Government did little to adopt these words of wisdom, and it was to be a decade before the word 'privatization' surfaced again.

Sidney joins the stags

'Tell Sid'
– A commercial on British television plugging the British Gas issue

'The Gas Bill spells catastrophe for the consumer just so the government can raise a fast buck for temporary, short-term tax cuts'
– Dave Sirzaker, secretary of GUARD, during the gas unions campaign against privatization

THE FIRST GREAT privatization in the UK was that of British Telecom. When 50 per cent of the company was sold by the Thatcher Government in November 1984 it created the biggest company on the London Stock Exchange. It also introduced the public to a new and popular game – 'stagging'.

Stagging is when you buy shares in a float or new issue, often with borrowed money or money you do not have, with a view to an immediate capital gain when you sell your holding a few minutes, hours or days after acquiring it. With most new issues, this is a high-risk gamble. If the issue is popular, then there is big demand, particularly from overseas, and market-makers price the issue up.

But if the issue is a flop – as with the much-hyped British flotation of the cookie company Mrs Fields in 1986 – then the share opens on the first day of trading below the offer price. The stag then has only two choices: to take his loss or to hang in on the market in the hope that at sometime in the future the share will recover to show a profit. This could take years. The true stag grits his teeth and gets out.

For stags privatization has been a no-risk game. There has been money to be made by stagging almost all the issues. The only notable exception was the sell-off of the remaining government stake in British Petroleum, which coincided with a slump in oil prices and was, for timing reasons, a notable flop. (See Chapter 6). But anyone who watched television news and who had only a minimum amount of common sense could foresee this, and not apply for the issue.

The British Telecom issue was the first stag party – and by far the greatest. Within 24 hours the price had risen by 90 per cent, and many people gratefully disposed of the maximum 800 shares they had been allocated. Around one billion shares changed hands on that first day.

Although making multiple applications was strictly forbidden – and those seeking shares had to sign a declaration agreeing to be bound by the condition that they had made only one application – the accountancy firm Peat Marwick discovered 6,000 forms filled in by those who had already applied. Their applications were, of course, ignored, although, mysteriously, only ten were prosecuted. Two Conservative MPs made multiple applications.

One of them, Keith Best, MP for Anglesey for eight years, was charged with dishonestly attempting to obtain 2,400 BT shares by deception, using variations of his name as well as different bank accounts and addresses on the application forms. As a barrister who signed the declaration, he must have known this was illegal.

One reason why British Telecom was such a great success for the stags was because the organizers of the sell-off managed to create a great sense of scarcity. This involved putting together a carefully developed strategy and implementing it with a public awareness campaign. David Clementi of the merchant bank Kleinwort Benson recalls:

For the banker the principal challenge was its sheer size: 50.2 per cent of the business was sold for about £4 billion. It was seven times bigger than any previous British share issue, and many times bigger than any offering in the United States. It represented the total amount which the major UK institutions had invested in the equity market over the previous two years.

For an issue of such a size to be successful, new marketing techniques and an innovative offer structure were necessary. The underlying strategy which was developed was not simply to maximize capacity, but also to encourage a sense of competition between the sources of demand in different markets, and to create a sense of scarcity.

Clementi led the strategy team, and targeted four markets: the big investment institutions; the British public; employees of British Telecom; and overseas institutions, mostly in the United States, Europe and Japan.

With the institutions, it was not enough to go in for the usual round of dinners and lunches with fund managers, although this was one important task for the Kleinwort Benson team. Clementi approached the issue from the other end, by encouraging BT to be open with stock-market analysts, whose research reports provided a useful catalyst for the market. By the time this part of the work was over, there was hardly a relevant senior fund manager who had not read a dozen BT reports, attended several round-table briefings and visited BT top executives.

The general public was targeted through advertising and public relations campaigns. The advertising campaign cost £12.4 million alone. A cartoon character, Busby, started to appear on television. Telephone subscribers, most of whom probably believed that British Telecom was just a branch of the Post Office, suddenly became aware that it was being run as a business. The more investment-minded members of the public began to read about British Telecom in papers like *The Observer* and the *Daily Telegraph*, and in journals like *Investors Chronicle*.

Local bank managers, share brokers and other financial intermediaries found themselves invited to British Telecom regional
roadshows, most of which were a great success.

Employees were targeted not through the union, the traditional conduit of the past, but direct. The offer was made
particularly attractive to them by offering them priority status
and a discounted share price, and, despite the hostility of union
leaders and most Labour MPs, was supported by 96 per cent of
the workforce, which decided it could not look a gift horse in
the mouth.

One innovation made by Clementi – and copied in every
privatization since – was the publication of a 'pathfinder'
prospectus. Although expensive to produce, this document
contained a wealth of information in simple language intelligible
to a *Daily Mail* reader as well as a student of the *Financial Times*.
It was available to anyone who sought it, and was advertised in
the major newspapers and on television.

Those who studied the prospectus carefully – particularly
professional market analysts – were able to frame the questions
that any investor should ask him- or herself before committing
funds long-term. The valuable information contained in it bode
well for future shareholder enlightenment, and we looked forward to British Telecom and other privatized bodies becoming
more open than they had been. Alas this was not to be. The
newly-privatized corporations made cosmetic improvements
and added gloss to their annual reports, but were no less frugal
with information than they had been in the past.

· 4 ·

How they did it

'This business is a romance'
– Lord King of Wartnaby, chairman of British Airways

ON A CRISP January day in 1987, the chauffeur-driven Jaguar of the crusty but amusingly ascerbic chairman of British Airways, Lord King of Wartnaby, curved into the forecourt of Lancaster House in London with all the style of a visiting head of state attending a Commonwealth Conference.

Inside, instead of robed African leaders bowing graciously to the sovereign, were several dozen women flight attendants, picked for their charm and poise, handing out canapés and the best French champagne to a large turnout of journalists, merchant bankers, stockbroking analysts and an assortment of camp followers.

At the meeting, to launch the pathfinder prospectus for the privatization of British Airways in February of that year, the Secretary of State for Transport, John Moore, was at pains to reinforce the message that had already been in the Sunday newspapers, as purveyed by merchant bankers from Hill Samuel, advisers to the government. 'This is not one for Sid,' said Moore, 'this is more for the professional investor. I expect that this issue will be taken up largely by those who already own shares.'

From the platform, Lord King, who had been brought in by Margaret Thatcher to chair the airline at a time when Americans, at least, half-believed BA stood for 'bloody awful', winced. You did not have to be an astute observer to appreciate that not only was Lord King in fundamental disagreement with the minister, but was also absolutely determined to prove him wrong. But the chairman, a former master of the Belvoir Hunt, one of the most famous in rural England, was too wily a fox to fall foul of a member of the Cabinet, so he remained silent.

Soon the party spilled over into a marquee in the garden of the Palladian mansion, and more champagne corks popped. The British Airways brass band struck up *Rule Britannia* and *Land of Hope and Glory*. Then, at a precise moment timed to coincide with the flight overhead of a Concorde inbound for Heathrow, Lord King released thousands of red, white and blue balloons which swirled into the cold morning air and floated gently away towards Westminster.

An hour later, King, British Airways chief executive Sir Colin Marshall and their posse of public relations and security men were on their way to Heathrow Airport to board a special Boeing 737 flight to Belfast. At Aldegrove, the chairman slipped his security men and strode purposefully to the gentlemen's toilet, where he was overheard making some choice remarks about politicians and civil servants.

Downtown at the Europe Hotel, there was time for some quick interviews with Ulster journalists before a 90-minute road show for financial advisers, bank managers and institutional investors. Then it was back to Aldegrove for a flight to the East Midlands, a drive home to Leicestershire, and then another day of road shows in Birmingham and Manchester.

These road shows followed a familiar pattern. First, an expensively-produced video about the self-styled 'world's favourite airline', featuring pearl-grey 747s banking in the clouds to the sound of ghetto-blaster music. Then a talk, illustrated by slides, from the men from Hill Samuel, followed by a few homilies from Lord King. The evening – or lunch-time – was rounded off with a buffet feast and champagne. Following a punishing schedule, King and Marshall visited Aberdeen, Glasgow, Edinburgh, Newcastle and Leeds, before setting off by Concorde for the United States. On Thursday 15 January they took in Boston and New York. Friday took them to windy Chicago, and then down to Florida. Another Concorde flight back to London, and it was on to Geneva for breakfast, Zurich for lunch and London for supper.

The purpose of the hyperbole and razzmatazz was to per-suade professional investment institutions, and wealthy individ-uals, that British Airways would be a sound investment. At least, that was the unofficial purpose, for share-pushing is strictly illegal, especially in privatization issues. Officially, the purpose of the road shows was to throw more light on Britain's state airline, so that advisers and institutions could make sound recommendations or decisions.

The run up to privatization for British Airways had not been easy, and, as it was fattened up for the private sector, the airline encountered several problems, one of which had delayed the float. British Airways had been involved in American litigation over competition on the North Atlantic which had led to the demise of Laker Airways; the possibility of an expensive legal action had to be removed before its shares could be sold. Moreover, passenger traffic between the United States and Britain had fallen dramatically as Americans cancelled their holiday bookings in Western Europe following the US action against Libya and the fear of reprisals, and also the movement to the west of the radioactive cloud from Chernobyl.

British Airways responded with a vigorous and successful marketing campaign, but the government still felt that most of the issue should be for institutions, rather than individuals. Almost half of the 720.2 million shares on offer at £1.25 each were therefore reserved for British institutions, and placed with them prior to the float. Another fifth were placed with insti-tutions in Japan and Switzerland, or offered to the public in North America. Ten per cent or more were allocated to BA on concessionary terms, which left less than a third of the total allocation for private investors. It proved not to be enough, but the Government did invoke contingency arrangements to claw back 20 per cent of stock from institutions if the offer was over-subscribed, which it was.

The public liked British Airways, and they were right. Over a million people bought shares, confounding the commentators and the Government.

· 5 ·

In search of Sid

'I have no doubt that the future commercial success of Britain will greatly benefit from the ownership of this company being spread among its employees, managers, the pension funds and the individual investors'
– David Hunt, Junior Energy Minister, on the privatization of British Gas

'What is wrong with being a dullish utility? I would rather be running that than be some fly-by-night whizz kid'
– Sir Denis Rooke, chairman of British Gas.

THE SELLING OF British Gas in 1986 was pure soap opera.

The £20-million campaign started simply enough, although, to those of us who have lost working hours waiting at home for the gas man to turn up, the television spots showing him hurtling around Britain lighting clifftop gas beacons to warn off a latter day *Armada* did strain the credibility. To the purists, it was also extremely misleading: British Gas only employs one lamplighter, whose job it is to light the gaslamps in London's legal quarter of The Temple.

As the process wore on, it also became clear that whatever nationalistic fervour this concept was designed to foster, those managing the flotation had no such feelings – for they were simultaneously busy canvassing potential overseas predators to buy substantial chunks of the issue.

The soap did not really begin until half-way through the campaign, when full-page advertisements in the national newspapers began appearing featuring a character called 'Sid'. At the top of the page, in relatively small print, the copy told readers to 'look out for British Gas prospectuses [sic] and application forms in banks'. But most of the advertisement was taken up with a handwritten scrawl, 'Tell Sid'.

As the campaign developed, policemen were seen looking for the wretched Sid under park benches, behind bushes, or wherever else someone without a ha'pence to his name to buy a newspaper might be lurking. The implication, presumably, was that anyone, however poor, however eccentric, should consider an investment in British Gas. It also seemed to me that the Government wanted older people to buy gas shares, for Sid ceased to become a fashionable name after the end of the Second World War. Nor did the television campaign manage to achieve for Sid what *Neighbours* did for Kylie.

But as the campaign wore on (reaching, according to the campaign directors, all but two per cent of the adult population) so interest grew. Would we ever get to see slippery Sid? The popular newspapers began to treat it as a 'Who killed JR?' mystery. But, wisely, Sid was never identified. In the final days, the last commercial was not dissimilar to an episode from Shakespeare's *Macbeth*. There was a grey-green afforested Scottish hillside, and a swirling wind. A tortured voice called, as from the grave, 'Sid, Sid, Siiidd'. But all we saw were the scudding clouds, and a shape, like Banquo's ghost.

Although the British Gas privatization was later to be dwarfed by the sale of the water industry and electricity, at the time it was the biggest share offering the world had ever seen – and certainly the most ambitious. No effort was spared to try to meet the Government's target of more than four million shareholders for British Gas, nearly twice as many as the record two and a quarter million who had turned out to buy British Telecom. The goal was also to turn into shareholders as many of the corporation's 90,000 employees and 13 million customers as possible. To widen the public appeal of gas, all investors could, if they wished, apply for only 100 shares, requiring a deposit of £50, compared with the minimum investment of £260 required to buy into British Telecom. There was also a special reduced scale of dealing commissions, to enable those who wanted to trade their allotments to do so at a much-reduced rate of commission. Other special deals and incentives were given to customers and employees, as we shall see later. Moreover, 40 per cent of the stock was reserved for the private investors, giving them equal treatment with institutions – a sensible move which, alas, has not often been followed in subsequent privatizations.

By an odd quirk the gas campaign did wonders for the newly-privatized British Telecom. Those seeking information had to telephone a number in Bristol, an expensive long distance call for all but a minority. Over five million did so, and towards the end of the publicity drive, individuals were applying for prospectuses at the rate of 17,000 a day. More than 3,500 Sids applied for prospectuses – but then so did 23 Fidos and one Donald Duck.

The campaign pre-occupied a large percentage of the staffs of the Department of Energy and British Gas for over a year. It also required the services of thousands of people in three merchant banks, five firms of solicitors, four firms of stockbrokers, four international investment banks, two firms of consultants, two advertising agencies, two public relations firms and one clearing bank.

Almost as much effort went into securing the interest of overseas investors as to flushing out Sid. As advisers to the British Government on the privatization of British Gas, Rothschilds did not want a repeat of the British Telecom float, whereby overseas institutions which were allocated shares dumped them on the markets at the first opportunity. The merchant banker Tony Alt made a point of trying to find genuine buyers, rather than stags. 'I want to make sure managers work to see the shares do not all end up in a few hands,' Alt said at the time. Alt and his team travelled extensively to find these buyers, as well as briefing droves of international energy analysts visiting London. I visited a couple of these briefings, and it was an impressive performance.

Centre stage in the long run-up to privatization was Sir Denis Rooke, chairman of British Gas, testy, opinionated and often contemptuous of politicians, civil servants, public relations flacks and the City. He once said to me that people in the City knew 'a lot about very little', and that 'what goes on each day on the Stock Exchange is of no relevance whatsoever to everyday life in industry'.

Rooke disliked appearing at the road shows – 'It's too late to turn me into a performing flea,' he used to say. When he could summon up the patience to talk to journalists, Rooke made it plain he thought privatization was a massive diversion from running the business, and that both the company's time and his own would have been better spent selling gas, not the company, and that his duty was to the public, above all. At its best, privatization was a 'bit of politicians' nonsense'.

Rooke, a mechanical and chemical engineer, had worked his way up through British Gas for 37 years, from the days when it produced gas from coal in smelly and unpleasant plants to be found on the outskirts of every town through its period of modernization, to the huge project whereby the whole of Britain was converted from town gas to natural gas piped in from the North Sea. He was regarded by many in Westminster and Whitehall as cantankerous. One Tory MP was quoted by the *Sunday Times* as calling him 'an entrenched and bigoted champion of monopoly privilege'. But he was also held in respect, even awe, and he always managed to meet performance targets, even those he had billed as impossible.

By the time the doors were closed on the late-comers rushing with their application forms into branches of the National Westminster Bank on the morning of 3 December, more than four and a half million had applied for gas shares, easily beating the Government's target, and almost doubling the number that had taken up the British Telecom issue. The offer had been four times over-subscribed, making the newspaper commentators who had predicted a failure look extremely foolish.

The forms of those who had pre-registered were taken to

computer terminals, and operators entered the reference numbers and the quantity of shares sought. Only the forms of those
using newspaper clips or making late applications had to be
dealt with manually. In previous privatizations, most of the
paper work had been done manually. Not only was this inefficient, but when, as in the case of the Trustee Savings Bank float
in 1986, the advisers balloted out only half of the total number
of public applicants, it chose to do so crudely by throwing out
half of the bundles and allocating shares to those left. This,
understandably, caused some acrimony.

All those who had made British Gas applications for 400
shares or less received a full allocation. Most other applications
were heavily scaled down: for example, those who had asked for
2,000 only received 800; those seeking between 15,000 and
100,000 received only 10 per cent of their application; and those
after more than that received only 5 per cent.

When trading began, the shares opened at a 12 and a half-
penny premium (the price of one share was £1.35), making it
clear that the Government and its advisers had judged the issue
exactly right. This did not stop Labour's Tony Blair accusing
the Government of throwing £600 million worth of taxpayers'
money away by under-pricing the shares. Neither did it stop the
Government's Energy Minister, Peter Walker, from claiming
British Gas was 'now run by five million families around the
UK, and not by some politician like Tony Benn'.

Sir Denis Rooke did not seem so sure: 'The company will be
run in the same way in the private sector as it was as a
nationalized industry,' he said.

And so it was.

· 6 ·

BP: the one that fizzed

BY EARLY 1987 the British Government had seen through three major privatizations – those of British Telecom, British Gas and British Airways – and the time seemed right to step up the programme and make some more money with which to reduce the public sector borrowing requirement. The timing was not right for another major sell-off. Ministers knew water would be controversial and require very careful preparation; British Rail and British Coal were not in fit condition; and electricity had the complication of the unpredictable value and liability of the nuclear power industry.

The obvious choice was for the Government to sell its remaining stake in British Petroleum. In 1979 and 1983 it had previously and successfully disposed of 18.5 per cent of BP by selling shares to institutions. The price of oil had now recovered from the lows prevalent at the time of the collapse of the OPEC oil cartel. Now was the time to allow the public to get a share in one of Britain's biggest companies, and one of the world's top oil corporations.

The Government appointed as its adviser the energetic Michael Richardson, head of corporate finance at NM Rothschild, and a veteran of privatization issues. Richardson had handled the gas privatization with skill and aplomb, and had told ministers that he believed he could get the cost of the final BP sale down by squeezing the underwriters' fees. This was a message which went down well with the Chancellor of the

Exchequer, Nigel Lawson, who had been heavily critical in previous flotations of the fees paid to the City.

On 18 March the Government announced it would sell its remaining stake in BP as if it were a privatization issue. The exercise looked pleasantly easy and uncomplicated: BP shares were trading buoyantly on the world's sharemarkets, and the only debate seemed to be over the price at which they would be made available when the float was to take place in the Autumn.

Then BP threw a rather large spanner into the works. The company owned a majority stake in the United States giant, Standard Oil of Ohio. Things were not going well there, and major changes in operations in Cleveland were needed. In the run-up to full privatization it knew it would have to disclose the problems to the public, face unpleasant criticism and cross-questioning, and incur opprobrium which might well prove a serious handicap to privatization. But to defer dealing with the problems of Standard Oil of Ohio until after full privatization would be to make matters worse. BP directors decided on the inevitable: to purchase the shares in Sohio the company did not already own.

The cost of doing this was a substantial $7,400 million, and BP needed a rights issue in order to finance it. Normally this would not have been too difficult – and world stock markets were booming at the time. At BP, some saw the pending privatization as a problem, but government ministers perceived it differently and thought of it as an opportunity for greater glory. So the Government bought up BP's rights issue, and rolled it into a much bigger privatization package.

That Summer, at Rothschild's headquarters at St Swithin's Lane in the City of London, Michael Richardson found little time for holidays as he set about the pleasant business of finding underwriters for the BP float. There has never been much difficulty in finding underwriters for privatization issues, because of the low risk. The role of the underwriter is – in return for fees and concessions such as discounted stock – to guarantee to buy up in its own right any shares not taken up by the public or others with whom they have been placed.

Two billion BP shares were to be sold. Half of them would go to private investors at a fixed price; the remainder would be available to British and overseas institutions at an auction. As an international giant, BP wanted its shareholders to be scattered across the globe, so underwriters were appointed in Europe, Japan and North America.

On the morning of 14 October, Richardson went to Nigel Lawson's office in the Treasury. The two men discussed the sharemarkets and current trends. That morning's *Financial Times* showed that BP had closed the night before at £3.62. Both Lawson and Richardson shared the same aim: they wanted the issue to be a success, politically for the Government and financially for the City. The issue price was settled at what was thought would be an attractive £3.30.

Back at St Swithin's Lane, Richardson called a meeting of those institutions interested in underwriting the issue. Sixteen turned up: Barclays de Zoete Wedd, Baring, British Linen Bank, Charterhouse, County NatWest, Hambros, Hill Samuel, Kleinwort Benson, Lloyds Merchant Bank, Robert Fleming, Samuel Montagu, Morgan Grenfell, Schroders, Standard Chartered, TSB and Warburg.

After being sworn to secrecy and told the price, each was invited to tender their bid privately. This was a variation on paying the underwriters a fixed fee, as had been the case with British Telecom. The average commission came out at a very low 0.018 per cent, tiny compared with the standard 0.5 per cent. But those present hoped to make more money by selling the issue to sub-underwriters – the investment institutions – at a price above the £3.30 at which it was being offered to the public. Within 24 hours they had done so: more than 400 institutions had snapped the shares up, acting as sub-underwriters to the underwriters who had been only too pleased to sign the contracts put in front of them in Rothschild's offices. Richardson could relax.

Most people in southern England will remember the next evening, 15 October 1987. A hurricane, a phenomenon virtually unknown in Britain, swept across Wessex and the Home Counties, uprooting trees and telephone wires, tearing off roofs and chimney pots, causing tens of million of pounds worth of damage to homes and cars, and plunging public transport and other utilities into chaos. Most families in the London commuter belt woke on the morning of 16 October to a tearing sound – like sheets of yarn being ripped apart. The sound was that of splintering wood, as trees buckled before the gales.

Very few people made it to the office that 16 October. Most trains were not running: too many trees blocked the lines. I was called by my son's boarding school in East Sussex and asked to collect him because the building was without heat, light or power. Somewhere between Goudhurst and Hawkhurst – attempting to find my way at dusk through lanes blocked by fallen oaks – I heard an item at the very end of a BBC news bulletin. Almost as an afterthought, the announcer said that in Wall Street the Dow Jones Industrial Average had fallen by 100 points in its first hour of trading.

No one gave a thought to BP's privatization – except, of course, Michael Richardson who, like many of those living in town, had made it to the office. Over the weekend he made contact with those in the Treasury and elsewhere who still had telephones that worked or who were not trying to patch up their homes. But there was little they could do. On Monday 19 October, Richardson's worst fears were realized: BP's share price fell below the offer level, closing at £3.17. Unless the markets turned up, the privatization would be a shambles, and his name would be mud with those who had staked their money on BP.

But the world's great stock-market meltdown had begun. Trading was all one way. By the night of Monday 19 October, the markets had gone into free fall, and the greatest stock-market crash in history was to take place. The Dow Jones Industrial Average shed 508 points. As Richardson was to say later, with characteristic understatement: 'That made me very pessimistic.'

The BP privatization was doomed.

7

The secret sweetener

*'I am very proud to have completed the transaction, and I have a completely
clear conscience about it'*
– Lord Young, after it had been made known that as Secretary
for Trade and Industry he had offered sweeteners to British
Aerospace to persuade it to privatize Austin Rover

THERE WAS ONCE a time when government ministers were
expected to behave with the utmost rectitude so far as public
money was concerned. All dealings of the late 60s involving
public money were faithfully and accurately reported to Parliament. Indeed, at the time of the giant OPEC surpluses, when
government ministers of all hues and from many countries were
beating a path to the Arabian Gulf to attempt to secure trade or
contracts for their industrialists, there was much pious condem-
nation of those who agreed to pay commission to effective
Middle Eastern intermediaries.

One sign as to the extent to which the former punctilious
standards had slipped came with revelations, at the end of 1989,
that Lord Young, as Secretary for Trade and Industry, had
actually sought to conceal from Parliament, the public and the
European Commission the fact that the Government had
secretly made tax concessions and supplied subsidies to British

Aerospace worth £48 million to encourage it to take over the only British volume car manufacturer, Austin Rover.

Lord Young's secret sweetener was only one aspect in which the privatization of the last remnants of the British-owned motor industry was conducted very differently from other privatizations.

Ever since taking office as Prime Minister, Mrs Thatcher had longed to rid the Government of the burden of one of Britain's greatest post-War industrial failures: the British Motor Corporation, which formed the basis of British Leyland, which in turn begat Austin Rover. So distasteful did she find the huge sums of money provided by successive Labour and Tory Governments to prop up this ailing dinosaur that she referred to it almost every time she was questioned in Parliament about alleged misuse of taxpayers' money.

More than any other minister, except perhaps the then Chancellor of the Exchequer, Nigel Lawson, Mrs Thatcher realized that no amount of calf-fattening, public relations antics or appeal to national pride would persuade the British public to swallow British Leyland. There was no price at which the shares could be sold.

It was not ever thus, as any reading of the biography of the great Lord Nuffield will indicate. Prior to the Second World War, Britain had an envied and wide marque of cars. There were the Austin Sevens and the Morris Eights, to be sure, but there were also the MGs, Wolseleys, Rileys and Triumphs. And there were the cars from the company founded by Lord Rootes: Hillmans, Sunbeams and Singers, all under British ownership.

In the 50s came the love affair with bigness. The Hillmans, Singers and Sunbeams hung together for a while under the careful eye of Lord Rootes, but they eventually fell prey to a disastrous takeover by Chrysler, the US corporation, which in turn sold its British car manufacturing operation to Peugeot. The others were swallowed up inside the British Motor Corporation, which proceeded to strip each of the marques of any of the individuality which had earned them the love and respect of the British motorist. Even when Alec Issigonis, the brilliant engineer, invented the Austin Mini, thus enabling the group to survive a little longer than it might otherwise have done, the visionaries then running BMC produced it in five faces, bolting hideous Wolseley, Riley and Vanden Plas façades to an otherwise attractive, if utilitarian body.

The British Motor Corporation became British Leyland when it swallowed up the Triumph Motor Company and the Leyland commercial vehicles group. The failures of British Leyland, headed by Sir Donald Stokes – later to receive a peerage for his efforts – were to provide the Japanese and European car makers with an unprecedented opportunity to penetrate the United Kingdom market.

British Leyland had, by virtue of the large number of marques in its franchise, half a dozen or more dealers in every major British town. Stokes' management decided this was too many, and the BL dealership was awarded to the largest. This left several disenfranchised dealers without new cars to sell. So when Otto Botnar, a canny German-born businessman, went the rounds offering the Datsun franchise for Japanese-built Nissan cars, there were grateful takers in every town. Soon Datsun had 10 per cent of the British car market – Renault, Fiat and Volkswagen also moved in. By the mid-70s, the majority of private individuals – that is, non-fleet buyers – were choosing non-British cars, and British Leyland was on the road to bankruptcy.

It was saved by the Wilson Government's National Enterprise Board: a body set up by Labour to achieve the opposite of privatization. Its objective was to enable Britain to achieve what Wilson, in a flight of fancy, liked to call a 'white-hot technological revolution' – to push promising new enterprises that were starved of capital because of the supposed short-termism of the City of London, and to save from collapse those whose survival was deemed to be in the national interest. Such a board, called 'Statsforetag', upon which the NEB was modelled, had worked well in Sweden. But in Britain it foundered, mainly because it became the playchild of socialist theorists, pushing investments in such doomed enterprises as the Meridien motor-cycle co-operative.

The Wilson Government bought most of the shares of British

Leyland, injected over £2 billion of taxpayers' money into it, and appointed the South African-born chairman of Chloride, Michael Edwardes, as chief executive officer to sort out the mess. Though a tougher manager than Stokes, Edwardes' reign was a mixed blessing, and when his term was up he moved on to another salvage operation, Dunlop.

Edwardes did, however, pull off the one deal which enabled BL to survive: one Christmas he left the family celebrations and flew to Tokyo to persuade Honda to invest heavily in the company, and to engage in a joint venture to build new models in Britain. Such a move was not popular in some circles: it was seen as selling out to the Japanese. But given that the British Government was by this time already enticing Nissan to a greenfields site in County Durham, Edwardes' move was a strategic necessity.

Honda's participation in BL – later to change its name to Austin Rover – paved the way for a return to respectability, the company becoming attractive enough to gain the attention of British Aerospace. Rod Young's Sweetener provided the extra incentive for BAe to take the company over.

8

Ports for sale

A TREAT FOR a Cockney schoolboy in the 50s was a trip on a passenger ship, the *Eagle*, which on each Summer's day slipped its berth in the Pool of London, below London Bridge, and steamed down the Thames. Tower Bridge would open, like a great medieval drawbridge, and then the ship would glide slowly past Millwall Docks and the Isle of Dogs where even larger vessels were tied up. While their masters and crew were sinking pints of beer in historic public houses like the 'Prospect of Whitby', freight of every kind was being unloaded on the wharves: bananas from the Canary Isles, teas from India, timber from Finland, dairy produce from Australia and New Zealand, spices from the Caribbean.

Further east, at Tilbury, were huge passenger ships, and more freighters, many of them loading British exports for other parts of the world. Out in the estuary, between the Isle of Grain and Southend, steamers of every size plied their trade, carefully navigating the mud-banks. By contrast to this living geography lesson, the end of the trip, Margate pier, was a bit of a let-down, it being just another dreary seaside resort. Children were taken on similar trips down Southampton Water or the Mersey to see trade in action.

Fifteen years later, these nationalized ports were all but dead, killed off by the policies of the very party that represented most of the people who worked in them, or on the ships that served them. In introducing the National Dock Labour Scheme

(NDLS), the Labour Government had the best of intentions. Dockers had been employed under conditions that would not have been acceptable in any other industry. Few, if any, of them had permanent jobs. Those who wanted to be considered for a day's stevedoring would turn up when a ship was due to dock, and take his chance that his uplifted hand would be spotted by the person handing out the work. Anyone with brawn was welcome, but work today was no guarantee of work tomorrow. Anyone injured or sick returned home to nurse their ailments without either sympathy or compensation.

The National Dock Labour Scheme spelt the end of casual labour in the ports. Instead, control of pay and conditions was placed in the hands of local boards which consisted of trades union representatives from the Transport and General Workers' Union and port employers. Most work was reserved for registered dock workers, who obtained a pass or 'ticket' entitling them to a job on the wharves.

It was not long before this system was abused and fell into disrepute. Those retiring or giving up the job 'sold' their tickets to union-nominees, or passed them on to their sons. Overmanning was endemic: men would go home after a day's idling on full pay. Work habits became as slipshod as the 'Spanish labour practices' in the Fleet Street printing industry – practices broken by Rupert Murdoch installing, ironically, a highly-automated new factory in the deserted wastes of Wapping, once the liveliest part of the London docks.

When ships became larger and many loads went by container, the unions opposed containerization because it meant less work for their members, though feather-bedding continued on a wide scale. This led shippers to evacuate the docks. Rotterdam, in The Netherlands, and Antwerp, in Belgium, took over the role once held by the Thames, Liverpool and Southampton, and cargoes were transhipped from these Continental ports to smaller British docks like Felixstowe.

This small Suffolk port, at the mouth of the River Orwell, became one of Britain's first and most successful privatizations. Today it carries 16 million tonnes of freight, and is the busiest port in the country.

While the National Dock Labour Scheme was in existence in 46 of Britain's 75 major docks, there was little chance of the rest of Britain's docks being privatized. Who would want them? But when he was Transport Secretary (1987–89), Paul Channon did undertake a drive to try and persuade entrepreneurs to follow the example of Felixstowe, and achieved a limited success. The small port of Boston, in unmilitant Lincolnshire, was sold by the local council for £4.1 million to two local companies who believed they could make a go of it.

In 1989, Sir Norman Fowler, who as a young reporter on *The Times* in the early 60s had reported on decasualization of the docks, and then rose through the Conservative ranks to occupy with distinction some of the senior offices of Government, managed to get the NDLS abolished. As Employment Secretary he outsmarted the dockers' unions, whose strike against the move crumbled. Within a few months, almost half of the workers registered under the NDLS were out of a job: the others found themselves working for a rapidly-expanding industry with potential.

It now seems likely that the major ports will all soon find their way into private ownership. Lower costs and new investment in technology are likely to attract back shippers from ports like Rotterdam, which though well-placed for the Rhine and for the industrial heartland of Europe, is now handicapped by congestion and the expensive job preservation schemes and high social security costs of The Netherlands. The old London docklands will never be returned to their former use, for the wharves have become high-cost flats for City yuppies, but places like Sheerness on the Isle of Grain, where entrepreneur Peter de Savary has major plans, look to have a bright future. Tilbury, Tees and Hartlepool, Hull, Grimsby and Southampton – all of them easily accessible to Europe – will probably be in private hands by the mid-90s.

Ironically Dover, once the prime candidate for privatization, is not likely to be on the initial list. Though closest to France and mainland Europe, it will have a hard job raising private capital when the biggest private capital venture of all – the Channel Tunnel – is on its very doorstep. But the Channel Tunnel is a different story – and deserving of a book in itself.

· 9 ·

Winning ways with water

'The water sell-off has seen the City pull the latest version of the three-card trick – rubbishing the issue in advance, forcing the Government to price it cheaply, and then piling in for easy profits. Chief dupe looks like being the taxpayer, who will net only around £500 million as first payment on an industry which had assets of £7.7 billion even on a limited historic cost accounting basis'
– Lex, the *Financial Times*

'I'm here because I'm needed by customers to ensure there is no exploitation'
– Ian Byatt, director-general of Water Services

IN WHAT PASSES for Summer in Britain it usually drizzles, and the leaden skies that often rain out Wimbledon, Henley or cricket test matches testify to the fact that the British are particularly well endowed with water. For most of this century, the British have held to the belief that their water should be free and plentiful, and, above all, that it was pure. Water, as children in schools across the country were told, only became suspect when you crossed the Channel. Once past Calais one drank only bottled water, or took care to boil the liquid on a primus stove.

The discovery in the late 80s that British water contained so many impurities that it was the most contaminated in the

European Community came as something of a shock to the average British family. They were even more horrified to discover that soon they would have to pay dearly for it. Households were urged to switch to showers, because it might become as expensive to run a bath as to heat the water.

That these discoveries should come about as the result of the proposed privatization of water was a remarkable commentary on the complete lack of public attention to the way in which the people had been supplied with nature's most basic requirement since the end of the parish pump. Of all the many authorities that form British public life, the ten water boards of Britain had almost entirely escaped scrutiny by both politicians and the media since the First World War. They lacked the glamour of the railways or aviation, although the engineering feats of Victorians like William Yarnold deserved greater recognition.

Ironically, much of Britain's water supplies had originally been taken into public ownership because of widespread public concern about standards of drinking water. In 1845, the Commission on the Health of Towns and Popular Places described water supplies in Britain as 'bad and frequently inferior in quality'. Three years later, 53,000 people died through cholera. The passing of the first Public Health Act led to the establishment of local health bodies with the power to supply water to their areas, provided that a private company was not already doing so.

By the start of the First World War, there were around 2,000 water companies in Britain, most of them controlled by local authorities, but some run independently. After the Second World War, substantial rationalization brought this down to 187, and then in 1973 the Water Act brought the industry within the ambit of ten regional authorities.

Even this did little to heighten public awareness of water. Because the charges levied on the average household were modest, few people troubled to question whether the bureaucrats that ran the authorities – under the supervision of water boards – were doing an adequate job.

There was the added complication that a large proportion of

the industry was already in private ownership, with about one-quarter of the population in England and Wales receiving their water from 29 statutory water companies, set up by separate Acts of Parliament.

Most people had no idea whether their water came from a private company or a public authority, and public awareness of the ten water authorities was sketchy. One explanation for this was the way they were structured. They did not conform to the geographical boundaries of most local governments; nor were their boundaries drawn in the same way as, say, regional health authorities. Rather, they were based on rivers, like the Thames, the Severn or the Trent, partly because the rivers were one of the major sources of domestic water. The authorities' power was, of course, not only restricted to supply of water: they were also responsible for sewage treatment, drainage, flood prevention and river management.

The people that ran the authorities were certainly not high profile. The nomination to a water board was seen as a sinecure: the brightest and best local councillors always aimed for education or planning committees.

But the inadequacies of the British water authorities – when fully revealed in 1989 by the Brussels-based European Commission – were almost sufficient to frustrate the aim of the Government to privatize water. The Environment Commissioner, the Italian Carlo Ripa di Meana, announced he would take the British Government to the European Court for failing to comply with EC water standards and for 'largely disregarding' a Commission directive published nine years earlier on water purity.

Ripa di Meana said British water posed a significant health risk. The level of nitrates in drinking water exceeded EC safety levels in parts of Britain inhabited by 800,000 people – including the whole of East Anglia – while 52,000 people in Scotland were slowly being poisoned by drinking water with a high lead content.

The EC study was reinforced by an investigation by Friends of the Earth which showed that nearly 300 water supplies in Britain contained pesticides above the maximum level allowed under the EC drinking water directive. Pesticide poisoning can occur very quickly and is detected from symptoms such as nausea, giddiness and restricted breathing. The Friends also estimated that about four million people in the country were drinking water that was infiltrated with nitrates.

Although the quality of drinking water was the principal focus of the Commissioner's complaint, the water industry faced other problems, too. Many of the sewerage systems in Britain were over-burdened or breaking down. Some of the sewers in Britain's major cities were crumbling, with rat-infested drains that had not been adequately repaired since the days of Queen Victoria.

It was obvious who was responsible for the years of neglect and irresponsibility: the British water authorities and Government parsimony. But rather than disband the 'terrible ten', the Government reinforced them as the privatized companies that would take the industry into the next decade, and made a bequest of over £5 billion to them to meet higher water quality and environmental standards.

£4.4 billion was paid over to the authorities to enable them to write off their debts to the Treasury. A further £1 billion in grants – known as the 'green dowry' – was made available to the industry to enable it to start investing for the future.

The industry estimated that to put things right – to improve drinking water and clean up rivers and beaches – it would cost at least £1.73 billion, double the rate invested in the 80s. Water authority chiefs argued that public expenditure cuts introduced by the Labour Governments of the 70s and continued by the Conservatives had made it impossible to maintain standards, and that the only way to meet the new environmental requirements, endorsed by a Prime Minister who had only recently reflected 'green' values in her public statements, was to increase the price of water to the consumer substantially.

Mrs Thatcher found herself painted into a most unattractive corner. If water prices were to rise after privatization by the percentages considered necessary by the authorities to pay for future investment, the Conservatives would carry the blame for them just as an election approached. On the other hand, to abandon water privatization would not only be to admit defeat, but the funds would have to be found from the Exchequer in any event to restore British water to its former high standards.

A damage limitation exercise was instituted. For most of 1989 a government minister, Michael Howard, engaged in bouts of verbal wrestling with the water chiefs. Howard was a bright lawyer who had been drafted in as Minister for Water Services after a short period as a junior minister attempting to come to grips with the financial services industry regulation in the Department of Trade and Industry.

It quickly became clear that he found the water authorities as thorough at bargaining as City institutions confronted with the costs of investor protection. It was not until early August, after most ministers and Whitehall permanent secretaries had departed for their summer holidays, that Howard found a way of achieving water privatization without committing British householders to yearly double-digit inflation in their water bills.

On the last day of July and the first day of August, Howard saw each one of the water authority chairmen individually. Over the preceding three months, consultants and merchant bankers armed with spreadsheets built up from information provided from the business plans of the authorities had convinced the Department of the Environment that writing off debt would be the most effective way of making water a sensible business proposition.

The water chairmen were haggling over two, related numbers. The first was the amount of debt to the Treasury the Department of the Environment was prepared to write off. In most cases all of the debt was written off, but in others this was not acceptable. In the end, the Anglian Water Authority became the only one saddled with a debt burden – of £148 million – but this was after the Government had struck more than £1 billion off its balance sheet. It had been treated more than generously.

Anglian also did well in the discussions over the second number, known as the 'K-factor'. This is the percentage in excess of the national inflation rate by which the water companies are permitted to raise prices. Anglian won a K-factor of

5.5 per cent for each year throughout the 90s, and will benefit also from a rapidly rising population.

Some authorities were offered relatively low K-factors – and rejected them. After some tough haggling Yorkshire accepted 3 per cent. Northumbrian told Howard that unless he came up with a better offer it could not recommend the privatization prospectus: Howard conceded a 7 per cent K-factor for the first five years of privatization. But Southern's William Courtney, having abandoned Cowes Week for the first time in 20 years, was the one who stuck it out to the last – well beyond the deadline Whitehall had set for agreement.

In the end Southern came out reasonably well: it won an injection of cash into its balance sheet to give it a £24-million surplus to enable it to get on with cleaning up its polluted beaches; and it achieved a K-factor of 5.5 per cent for three years, 3.5 per cent for a further two years, and then nil.

It was a good, if costly, victory for Howard. The water companies had, with the exception of Anglian, clean balance sheets, and the prospect of £7 billion of equity with which to face the future. The only outstanding matter was to get the issue price right.

WATER AS A PROPERTY ASSET

While government ministers and their City advisers haggled about the price, there were many in the Conservative Party who were still harbouring serious doubts about the wisdom of privatizing the nation's water supplies. Their number included those who had been very enthusiastic about other sell-offs. It had already been decided that water supplies in Northern Ireland and Scotland would remain in public ownership.

It was far from obvious both to them and the electorate why water had become a priority for the Government. Four years earlier, Thatcherites had seemed positively lukewarm about the concept, and it was only some determined lobbying by Roy

Watts, chairman of the Thames Water Authority, that persuaded ministers to go ahead.

Watts had been an abrasive and determined senior executive of British Airways, rising from the tough job of managing the airline's European division to becoming deputy chief executive. He – and the airline industry – had imagined that he would take over the top job and lead British Airways into the private sector. It was not to be. Mrs Thatcher chose one of her favourite figures from the private sector, John King, head of engineering group Babcock and Wilcox, to head BA. Watts was ousted and King replaced him with the man who had turned round Avis Europe, Colin Marshall.

Watts found himself in what many of his friends and admirers saw as a sinecure: the chairmanship of Thames Water. Because of their low profile, the water authorities seldom, if ever, generated much excitement. The public's only contact with them was the quarterly water supply invoice.

Watts saw things differently – certainly so far as Thames Water was concerned. The opportunist manager that had spotted good air route possibilities for the old British European Airways saw that Thames Water was sitting on one of the most valued assets in the Britain of the 80s: property. From Lechlade to Teddington, where the River Thames becomes tidal, there were locks, pumping stations, footpaths, gardens. Like British Rail's stations, these had huge development potential, not as office blocks, but as marinas and other centres of leisure serving the public. The same was true along the Thames' many tributaries. Then there was the river itself: popular in some key places, but generally under-utilized as a source of pleasure and as a means of transport.

Only privatization could release the value in these resources. Watts hired the services of an old journalistic acquaintance, former *Sunday Times* industrial editor Ian Coulter, who, by the mid-80s, had become a successful political lobbyist. Soon Coulter was at work, lunching with former colleagues and ministerial contacts.

At the same time, Watts took on the Government in an unusual and unexpected confrontation. The Thames Water board took exception to the proposed repayment to the Treasury of an extra £40 million in loans, and the consequent increase in domestic water charges of 10 per cent to cover it. He insisted that his authority would not repay the money unless the move was approved on the floor of the House of Commons.

The Government won the division, but not before 19 Conservative MPs, all supporting Watts, and many from the Thames Valley region, had defied the Conservative whips and crossed the floor of the House. Watts went public and said that there was 'considerable disquiet about the financial relationship between the Government and the water and other utility industries', and suggested Thames Water should pioneer water privatization.

Though many of the authorities were sceptical, they supported Watts' insistence that the concept of integrated river management should be retained. This concept was endorsed in a government White Paper in February 1986, which saw the public sector as being limited to flood protection and land drainage.

By now some stern opposition was emerging, particularly from the Country Landowners' Association and the Confederation of British Industry which argued that poachers (privatized water companies) should not also be gamekeepers (guardians of the environment). The lobbying intensified when, in May 1986, Nicholas Ridley replaced Kenneth Baker as Environment Secretary, and Ridley was won over.

Ridley proposed the establishment of a National Rivers Authority to mind the environment and regulate the water industry, as well as taking over many of the functions Watts had sought for the privatized water boards. He gave Patrick Brown, one of the most experienced privatization experts in Whitehall, the job of conducting the Environmental Department's first foray into privatization. And he informed the industry that the Government had decided all ten authorities would have to be floated together rather than separately, as many of them had wished. Whitehall believed it was important that each of the authorities be treated evenly, and that the best way of enabling the investing public to assess them as investments would be for all of them to be floated on the same day.

In many ways water privatization could not have come at a worst time. The public excitement created by the early sell-offs of British Telecom and British Gas had been replaced by a robust cynicism towards the City of London and the Stock Exchange in particular. The Big Bang of October 1987 had dealt individual investors a particularly severe blow. They discovered, almost overnight, that their business was not wanted by most of the major London sharebroking houses, who sparred among themselves to see who could pay young and inexperienced dealers the most money. Trading commission charges to the public went up, rather than down, while the face of the friendly stockbroker turned into a snarl when the Government introduced personal equity plans for individuals.

Families were told by their newspapers that shares were not for them, and that a safer form of investment than these PEPs would be unit trusts or insurance mutual funds. Many were persuaded by seductive advertising in the national press to abandon their privatized holdings for these collective forms of investment, unaware that the City's fund management groups had loaded its extra management and regulatory costs heavily on to these funds to the point where they were becoming singularly unattractive.

Then came Black Monday and the world's greatest stock-market crash, which could not have come at a worse time for one important privatization: the sale by the Government of its remaining shares in British Petroleum. As described earlier in this book, the sale turned out to be a disaster, for at the time of the offer the shares were priced higher than on the stock market. To the consternation of the City the Government went ahead with the sale, leaving the underwriters to pick up the pieces. If Sid decided to 'Be Part of It', as BP had advertised, then he was on to a loser.

Many commentators thought the climate – and public attitudes – bode ill for water. In the end, however, water was the second most popular privatization in Britain. Only the 1986 flotation of British Gas, which attracted four million applicants, exceeded the response to water, which drew 2.6 million applications. When dealings opened in January 1990 all the water companies were marked well up, while Northumbrian rose to nearly 70 per cent above its partly-paid price.

The public offer was more than four times over-subscribed, with applications for 2.86 billion shares chasing the 520 million that the Government had earmarked for private individuals. This meant that Howard had to activate the claw-back procedures and recover holdings pledged to the institutions acting as underwriters. As a result, by the time allocations were announced on 11 December, 47 per cent of the water issue was in private hands, 39 per cent with British institutions and 14 per cent with overseas institutions.

There were three reasons for the success of the water privatization. The first was the brilliant promotion campaign. Not only was it clever, but it was credible. In the final stages, the Government's lead adviser, merchant bank J Henry Schroder Wagg, was open and candid and kept Press and public extremely well informed, almost drip by drip.

Gerry Grimstone, the corporate finance director, and at one time the Treasury official in charge of privatization, showed no reluctance to go on television, and talked coherently and in language everyone could understand: a sharp contrast to the poor performance of those at the centre of some of the earlier privatizations.

The second reason was price; and the third was that rare vehicle in investment: a substantial local concern within which the public could identify and make a low-risk investment.

You would have had to be a family of aesthetics living in the country, declining to read newspapers or to watch television, and burning all direct mail, not to be aware of the water sale. Its slogan, 'You too can be an H_2Owner', was almost as well known as the catchy 'Tell Sid' campaign of British Gas. The ten water boards spent £20 million on television, poster and newspaper advertising; the Government spent the same on its own campaign.

The water companies' extravaganza did, of course, lead to

very substantial public criticism. The Independent Broadcasting Company logged 113 complaints about the use of ratepayers' money, but the television companies were delighted, as was the Press, which voiced very little adverse comment. What strained the credibility were the hypocritical statements by water company chairmen insisting that the advertisements were nothing to do with privatization, but had been placed simply to increase the public awareness of their activities. Given that Britain was in the midst of a rare dry summer, there was no shortage of information about water, only of the H_2O itself. And, as national advertisement managers of the major papers testified, previous press advertising by water authorities had been conspicuous by its absence.

But Schroders' Grimstone accurately observed that public criticism of waste of money would soon evaporate. As lead adviser, Schroders had come up with the idea that in order to be eligible for incentives, investors would have to pre-register. That gave it a good idea that whatever the media might claim, water privatization was popular. 'As the flotation got under way,' said Grimstone, 'people would start thinking about their wallets and concentrate on the merits of the individual companies up for sale.' (*The Economist*, 16 September 1989.)

That is exactly what they did. When the price was set, it was clear that this was going to be the most generous hand-out since British Telecom. By asking investors to pay only £1 per share, with two further instalments of 70 pence over an 18-month period, the Government was providing them with a one-way bet. The shares were bound to go up – and they did. And although the traditional City stockbroking houses made it plain that they would only deal in water shares for regular clients, the banks and building societies maintained no such restrictive practices, and were prepared to deal at reasonable rates. Barclayshare was charging a minimum commission of £12.50 for £1,000 worth of shares; Midland Stockbrokers charged a flat rate of £15 a family; while the Norwich & Peterborough Building Society beat them all with a £8 commission for up to four members of a household.

Finally, the fact that there were ten companies to choose from was very satisfying for the local investor. Each of the companies had their charms and attractions – as well as their disadvantages.

The high-profile Thames Water was billed as the best buy, partly because of its location in one of the most prosperous parts of the country, but also because the experienced Roy Watts was adopting an aggressive diversification strategy which aimed at half the profits coming from non-core business within five years. Even before the float Thames had bought a well-known international water treatment business.

Another favourite was Anglian, because of its high growth potential in the fastest-growing region in Britain, and because of its modern installations. However, Anglian is handicapped by the low rainfall in the region and the intensive cereal farming which has generated an unacceptable level of nitrates in the soil. On a par with Anglian was Yorkshire, whose chairman, Gordon Jones, was also a leader in the privatization negotiations, and which gave the appearance of being a soundly managed business.

At the other end of the spectrum were South West, serving a part of the country which has been repeatedly hit by drought and pollution, and North West, which has a backlog of problems left over from the industrial revolution, not least of which is the state of the polluted River Mersey and crumbling sewers in the major cities.

In between were Northumbrian, Severn Trent, Southern, Welsh and Wessex. Welsh Water is, in fact, governed by different rules from the rest: a takeover of the company is not possible even after five years unless 75 per cent of the shareholders agree to it. The attraction of water as an investment was like water itself – clean and reliable.

A CLEAN INVESTMENT

Just as a glass or two of water after a night-out can clear the system, so an investment in water is a perfect antidote to market hiccups. The core business is highly resilient to the ups and downs of economic cycles. Everyone needs water, and the new water companies have local monopolies in supplying it. The Government has also accepted that dividends should increase above the rate of inflation – guaranteeing that water is a safe investment, and one that will grow.

The British public were not the only ones to see the attractions of water as an investment. Across the Channel, French water companies – already enjoying a privatized system somewhat different from the United Kingdom one – were quick to move in on the industry.

In France, three-quarters of the water supply industry is in private hands, run mostly by five large and long-established companies. Three of these companies – SAUR, owned by the construction giant Bouygues, Compagnie Générale des Eaux, and Lyonnaise des Eaux – are among the largest listed companies on the Paris Bourse, and operate internationally with water plants on all continents.

Olivier Celier, international development manager of SAUR, uses a colourful metaphor to describe the activities of the big five. 'Put five rats in a cage and what do they do?' he asks, rhetorically. 'They try to get out of the cage.' Three of the groups now control 12 of Britain's statutory water companies, and after privatization, were building large stakes in the new operations.

It is unlikely that the growing French shareholdings will influence the way the water supply industry is run, because of the differences in the systems. In France, most treatment plants, pumping stations and pipes are owned by local municipalities, and the water companies compete amongst each other for long-term contracts to supply the water that flows through the pipes. In this way there is more competition between water companies: whereas in Britain the water companies have local monopolies.

But where the French companies have diversified is in services to households. Since water is metered, companies have a direct relationship with every home or business they serve. This has enabled them to think laterally and move from the water supply business to parallel developments – ranging from construction to cable television.

By the year 2000, the balance sheets of privatized water companies will look very different from those in 1990, the first year under the new order. Most of them will be diversified businesses, of which property, leisure, building and construction, cable television and telecommunications services will form the main branches. In Yorkshire, they are looking at power generation – from wind-power.

· 10 ·

Electricity powers up

'As privatizations go, this one looks more like a chain saw massacre. Even the liberals are beginning to be inhibited by what is happening in the United Kingdom'
– Pierre Delaporte, chairman of Electricité de France.

IF YOU COOK and heat your home with gas, use oil lamps to provide light and drive a car to work, you might be able to manage without electricity – just. You would not be able to use a vacuum cleaner or a washing machine, or watch television.

Life without electricity is grim, as I discover fairly regularly when wild swans fly into the overhead power lines near my home and create power cuts that extend up to eight hours. We shiver under candle-light and curse the power authority for not having the foresight – or the environmental spirit – to lay the cables underground.

Electricity is the most all-pervasive of the products or services provided by state-owned industry. Telecommunications, much of public transport, industry and information technology are all dependent on it. National economies are critically and directly affected by the price of power.

For this reason, and in theory at least, its privatization should be more widely discussed and more controversial than any other, even water. But as Britain moved towards selling off the family power supplies in 1990, there was virtually no serious debate – either in Parliament or on television – on either the issue or the consequences.

That this should be the case in a democracy was even more surprising, given that by disbanding the Electricity Council and the Central Electricity Generating Board, and replacing them with privately-owned corporations selling electricity to monopoly regional distributors, the British Government was carrying out one of the world's biggest-ever restructuring of an industry. Privatizing electricity was seen as inevitable – and, once again, the Thatcher Government appeared to be substituting a public monopoly with a private one. As before, the first casualty was competition.

Britain will not be the first country to have its supplies of electricity in private hands. In Japan, Tokyo Electric Power provides electricity to the Tokyo Bay area, is the largest private sector power company in the world, and is quoted on the world's major stock exchanges. Its share price is seen as an important barometer on the state of the Japanese economy. United States power utilities are also heavily-traded investment vehicles. There are more than 3,000 of them providing Americans with electricity, but they have no power to set prices.

On the face of it, the way electricity is being privatized in Britain is fairly sensible. There will be 19 new electricity companies. Two of them, Nuclear Electric and Scottish Nuclear, will remain in the public sector, for reasons I will explain later. Twelve companies will rise from the ashes of the present area boards, acting as distributors of power and as owners of the National Grid. Most of the electricity in the Grid will be generated by two large companies, National Power and PowerGen.

In a free market system, other companies, including those from across the Channel, should be able to supply power freely to the National Grid. National Power and PowerGen should be able to buy their raw energy supplies – coal, gas or whatever – from any source, preferably the cheapest. And the manufacturing industry – or office blocks – should be able to generate their own power, or buy from private generators.

That is not the way it will work in Britain. The Government has already forced National Power and PowerGen to buy the lion's share of their raw energy supplies from British Coal. This agreement will last at least until 1993. Steaming in coal from countries as far away as Australia or Poland would have been much cheaper, but Mrs Thatcher wants both to avoid another confrontation with the miners and to fatten up British Coal for its own privatization. The generators will also be obliged to purchase some of their power more expensively from nuclear power installations, and will be entitled to charge a levy on the customers. These two restrictions will ensure that electricity flowing into the grid will start by being unnecessarily costly.

Households and small businesses will have no choice but to buy power from the local monopoly company, at a tariff rate – a restriction that will stay in place until 1998 at the earliest. This means that the 12 new private distribution companies will have protection from most competition. After 1998, the generating companies will be able to take over their customers, but only to a limited extent. The National Grid, which the distribution companies will own, will also have the responsibility of pooling the supplies of electricity from the nation's 54,000 megawatts of power plant, with all area companies paying exactly the same amount for it. Thus, the area companies will never have to worry about creating power supplies, or investing capital to do it: whenever they need power the grid will always be there, and the customers will also always be there to pay the bills. If they do not, they will be cut off. It will be a nice cosy monopoly – and for fast-growing areas like East Anglia, a licence to make money. No wonder the institutions are enthusiastic.

NATIONAL POWER AND POWERGEN

The largest of the power generators in Britain is National Power, which seems to have been endowed by the Government with the best chance of making money. It already has more than half the generating capacity in England and Wales, and is run by John Baker, a former civil servant and, between 1986 and 1989, managing director of the Central Electricity Generating Board, the bureaucratic monolith that used to produce the nation's electricity.

To his credit, Baker looks towards shedding much of this bureaucracy. He has already cut out the inefficient and largely unnecessary regional tier of management, so that the managers of the power stations report directly to a board member. They and other senior managers have been put on performance-related pay. To Baker, power stations are profit centres, rather than cost centres.

Baker believes that competition with PowerGen will centre around efficiencies like this rather than price-cutting, claiming that output prices will be no more elastic than those of oil companies to petroleum retailers, with the final figure governed more by the cost of the raw material.

Since his company is obliged to buy so much fuel from British Coal, Baker sees changing the mix of raw energy supplies as one way to get costs down. This means using more natural gas, and National Power is seeking to build combined cycle gas turbine plants in Lincolnshire and East Anglia. When the limitations on imported coal are lifted, the company hopes to import up to ten million tonnes a year, using new privatized ports to do so.

PowerGen is a slightly different animal. Like Avis it likes people to believe that it 'tries harder'. It was hot off the mark by winning the contract to supply the new Toyota plant in Derbyshire – even before privatization. It has already commissioned from Siemens in Germany the construction of a 900-megawatt gas turbine-powered station on the Humber at Killingholme, is contracted with Atlantic Richfield to buy the entire output of the Pickerill field in the North Sea, and has joined with Conoco to build a 50-kilometre pipeline.

Its chief executive, Ed Wallis, gives the impression of a man not afraid to take risks, or use new techniques. One of these is to use, as a raw fuel, orimulsion – 70 per cent bitumen and 30 per cent water – which will be imported from Venezuela. 'We have a fuel burn in the first year which is 95 per cent British coal,' says Wallis. 'We believe that no private sector business can put all its eggs in one basket. We have got to achieve a better balance.'

Like National Power's Baker, Wallis has made PowerGen's 21 power stations profit centres, and ripped out layer upon layer of bureaucracy. 'We are going to be the UK's lowest-cost producer of electricity,' he proclaims.

It is the Government's intention that, apart from these two giants, there will be independent power generators, able to feed electricity into the National Grid. Corporations or consortia can apply to the Energy Secretary for permission to build large-scale generating plants from around 200 megawatts to over 2,000 megawatts. At the time of writing, 17 have done so, although only one has been approved. All of them have proposed to use gas as the energy source.

If National Power and PowerGen prove they can cut costs, then entering the market could be a high-risk business for the independent operator: it has to make a fine judgement on electricity demand; it has to make long-term contracts with suppliers of gas; the capital costs are high; and the four-year restrictions on competition will work to the advantage of the big two.

There may be a temptation for major gas producers to enter the market, but so far none of them have displayed much interest, preferring to remain suppliers.

There is also no reason why smaller independents should not enter the market, using renewable energy sources such as wave and wind power, and refuge burning. Denmark is just one European country using wind power for substantial amounts of local generation. Until oil and gas prices rise – and this seems likely in the mid-90s – it is unlikely that power generation from these alternatives will take off, although to date at least 300 schemes are on the drawing board.

NUCLEAR ELECTRIC AND SCOTTISH NUCLEAR

Nuclear power is an emotive issue, and the accidents at Three Mile Island and Chernobyl have deepened public suspicion. In Britain, the report of Professor Martin Gardner, linking ten cases of childhood leukaemia to the Sellafield reprocessing plant in Cumbria, has added to the concern. Nuclear power also suffered a severe setback with the reduction in real terms of energy prices following the OPEC hikes of the late 70s.

In 1989, the Government decided that electricity could not be privatized if the nuclear generation industry was included. Why it made this decision at such a late stage remains something of a mystery. Two years earlier, ministers had been told by the CEGB and its chairman, Lord Marshall, that the nuclear industry faced huge bills, running to billions of pounds, when the older Magnox stations were ultimately decommissioned and nuclear waste reprocessed.

So the industry was hived off into the state-owned companies, Nuclear Electric and Scottish Nuclear, which will have to pay these bills, most recently estimated at £13 billion. They will be part-financed by a levy, misleadingly called the 'fossil-fuel levy', which will add just over 10 per cent to electricity bills.

THE NATIONAL GRID

The 7,000-kilometre-long National Grid is – and will remain – a monopoly under the Government's plans, and will be responsible for co-ordinating all power stations with more than 100 megawatts capacity and for the flow of electricity to the 12 distribution companies in England and Wales. The Government seems determined not to have alternative networks – except in the case of very large plants being supplied from an adjoining generator.

A tight control is to be kept on the National Grid's costs, and its rate of permissable return is likely to be restricted. The way it will work is that each day the generating companies, led by

National Power and PowerGen, will tell the NG at what price they will supply electricity in each half-hour of the following day. National Grid will then select the cheapest generator able to fulfil demand, and add its own costs and profit when supplying to the distribution network.

Althought the National Grid will be owned collectively by the distribution companies, they will not be allowed to control its investment plans. Nor will they control its pricing, which will be set by the Department of Energy.

SELLING THE ELECTRICITY

At the sharp end of electricity privatization are the distribution companies, modelled on the former area boards, and with most of the same responsibilities.

Most people only come into contact with them if there is a power cut, if they visit a local showroom, when they pay their bills or when 'the man comes to read the meter'. This is likely to change radically as local companies seek more visibility with customers, and diversify into other businesses.

The 12 boards soon-to-become-companies, starting in London and moving clockwise around Britain, are: London Electricity, SEEBOARD, Southern Electric, SWEB, South Wales, Midlands, Manweb, NWEB, Northern Electric, Yorkshire Electricity, East Midlands Electricity and Eastern Electricity. Some are likely to move into telecommunications and some into cable television. All are likely to become much more aggressive in the white goods and appliance market. As with water, all are likely to attract investment from parallel industries, such as electrical retailers. Some are likely to enter the power generation market as independent suppliers.

SCOTLAND DOES IT DIFFERENTLY

In Scotland, as with education, the law and many other aspects of life north of the border, the method of privatization is totally different. The separation of power generation from distribution will not apply. Instead, there will be two full service companies, Scottish Power and Scottish Hydro-Electric. Each will produce, transmit and distribute power in Scotland – and because the Scots have an electricity surplus almost equal to their consumption, each will be able to sell power to the National Grid.

Scottish Power is attempting to expand south of the border: in the Spring of 1990, it tendered to build a new power station for the London Underground.

HANSON'S SPOKE IN THE WHEEL

Until the Summer of 1990, the Government had led people to believe that the privatization of electricity would be conducted much as other public flotations – with a pathfinder prospectus, and an offer price to members of the public underwritten by the institutions. There was no reason to believe that it would take a different course. During the second reading of the Electricity Bill, the junior minister at the Department of Energy gave an assurance that no single company would be allowed to own more than 15 per cent of any privatized power company.

But Lord Hanson, chairman of Hanson Trust, one of Britain's top ten companies, a major contributor to Conservative Party funds, and a man with a renowned reputation for making assets sweat, had other ideas. One May evening he was the guest speaker at the annual dinner of Rothschild's, held at Cliveden, the former home of the Astor family and the setting for the Christine Keeler affair with John Profumo which was to be the downfall of the Macmillan Government in the 60s. Hanson made a strong speech supporting Margaret Thatcher's Government, urging the City to 'rally round the flag'.

The next morning he and his long-standing partner, Sir

Gordon White, who runs the American side of the Hanson operations, had breakfast with one of the guests at the dinner, John Wakeham, the Secretary of State for Energy, and the man responsible for electricity privatization. Hanson suggested to Wakeham that instead of spending large sums of money in the City arranging a public float for PowerGen, the second of the two generating companies, the Government should sell it to him. The suggestion was not without its attractions to Wakeham. Although the Conservatives would immediately expect to come under fire for favouring one of the Party's strongest supporters and closest friends, it would remove one of the principle problems of electricity privatization: how to make two generating companies simultaneously and similarly attractive to investors? It would also save substantial expenses in underwriting, advertising and public relations – just the sort of costs that had been incurred in the case of British Gas and British Telecom and for which the Government had rightly been subjected to criticism. Under the Hanson proposal, a deal could be struck quickly and a major part of electricity privatized almost at a stroke.

It was nine weeks before Wakeham disclosed the proposal to an astonished House of Commons. On Monday 23 July, he rose to inform MPs that although the Government had 'made no final decision to proceed with a trade sale of PowerGen, I have a duty to the taxpayer to get a proper return from the sale of the electricity companies, and I therefore propose to pursue discussions with Hanson in parallel with pushing forward preparations for the flotation of PowerGen'.

After stating that the Government would have to consider other companies alongside Hanson on a tender basis – and would impose certain conditions and commitments – Wakeham concluded:

> The private sector has always thrived on competition to the benefit of customers, employees and shareholders. I believe Hanson's approach is a vote of confidence in a company which, however it is privatized, will be a major competitor in the new electricity supply market.

Inevitably there was an outcry from Labour. Gordon Brown, the opposition's spokesman on trade and industry, called for an investigation into what he dubbed 'privatization sleaze'. Neil Kinnock, the leader of the opposition, said the disclosure showed the 'sleaze and shadiness at the heart of the Government . . . there is private enterprise and there is looking after your friends; I think the country can tell the difference between the two'.

Wakeham's statement contradicted everything that had previously been said about the privatization of electricity. When asked about the previous assurance from his junior minister, Spicer, Wakeham replied blandly that when the assurance had been given the prospect of a trade sale had not been considered.

Two weeks earlier, Wakeham's advisers had dismissed speculation of a trade sale as 'nonsense', an example of the general contempt for the truth that is fairly widespread in senior Whitehall circles and amongst City advisers.

It is easy to see why Wakeham needed time to come clean about the Hanson offer. A trade sale could not have been further from the Government's supposed aims of privatization: the concept of a wider shareholding public – fair shares for everyone. It was just another cynical transfer of a public monopoly to a private one – the theme that has persisted through most British privatizations.

Wakeham's advisers used the time between the breakfast with Hanson and White and their public announcement to present the story in its most favourable light. Wakeham, it was said, was merely doing his public duty, by using the method most likely to raise the maximum amount of money for the taxpayer.

A few week's later, the Government abruptly dropped the idea of a sale of PowerGen to Hanson, and decided in favour of a public float in the traditional style. By then Saddam Hussein, the President of Iraq, had invaded oil rich Kuwait, sending energy prices soaring and plunging world stock markets into the biggest free fall since the Crash of 1987. The whole question of electricity privatization in 1990 was placed in doubt.

· 11 ·

The spoils of privatization

'It's a free world. If you do not want us to be paid at all, we will do some other job'
– Lord King, chairman of British Airways, at the company's annual meeting

'The British Gas issue is going to be the biggest national event of its kind ever seen'
– Tony Alt, director of the merchant bank N M Rothschild & Co

'The only thing that creates wealth in the world are things like fishing and farming and mining and taking resources and creating something. I understand that in the City they make a turn by shifting money from A to B, but if there wasn't someone out there getting dirty, the City wouldn't be there'
– Sir Denis Rooke, talking to the *Daily Telegraph*

WHEN LORD KING of Wartnaby was persuaded by Margaret Thatcher to take on the job of fattening up British Airways for privatization, he was offered – and accepted – an emolument of £160,000 a year. It was not a princely sum for a man who, as chairman of Babcock and Wilcock, had built up a very successful company. But by 1989, with the job accomplished and the airline turning in record profits of £268 million, King was earning £385,791, more than double the pre-privatization amount, and an increase of 116.6 per cent over the year before.

There is little doubt that among the principle beneficiaries of privatization have been those who have guided state-owned enterprises into the private sector. Lord King may have been the person treated the most generously, but most other senior managers have reason to be immensely grateful to the Government for the transformation in their lifestyles. Originally forced to live off the same kind of modest salary as the Prime Minister is paid, these tycoons now enjoy benefits comparable to those available in long-standing private corporations.

Generally, in these days of inflation, a senior executive in big business can expect to double his or her salary every ten years. A detailed study – *Does Privatization Work?* – by the London Business School in 1988 found that this is exactly what happened between 1979 and 1988 in nationalized industries like the Central Electricity Generating Board and the Post Office.

For newly-privatized industries it was a totally different story, where payments to the top people have tripled or even quadrupled. The average privatized director's fee rose from £33,000 to £90,000, while chief executive salaries rose from an average £47,400 to £164,300. Sir Denis Rooke, chairman of British Gas, saw his pay increase from £49,000 to a pre-retirement figure of £184,000. The job of running Britain's airports was only thought to be worth £37,000 in 1979; by 1988, the chairman of the British Airports Authority was getting £151,000.

Put another way, the salaries of chief executives rose by an average of 78 per cent in the year immediately after privatization, and by 250 per cent in real terms since 1979.

According to the London Business School study, executive directors also fared well, though on a more modest scale. The average pay of executive directors of £33,300 in 1979 had risen to £90,800 by 1988. The luckiest directors were those of British Airways (£142,000) and British Telecom (£112,000), compared with the luckless individuals in electricity supply who had to live off £56,000. But then, every dog has his day, and with electricity supply privatization, the first of the 90s, things will change for the Cinderellas of the power supply industry.

WHAT PRIVATIZATION HAS DONE TO PAY

Company	Top executive's pay (£s)	
	1979	1989
Amersham	31,000	90,000
BAA	37,000	151,000
British Airways	45,000	253,000
British Gas	49,000	184,000
British Telecom	na	198,000
Cable and Wireless	31,000	208,000
National Freight	44,000	143,000
Rolls-Royce	95,000	130,000
Not privatized		
British Coal	49,000	145,000
British Rail	54,000	90,000
Post Office	48,000	84,000

Source: London Business School

By comparison, the workers of newly-privatized concerns have not received anything like these benefits, or, in many cases, any benefit at all. However, they have done better than those who are still in the public sector, whose pay has become a major victim of a Conservative Government squeeze. Like their bosses, British Airways employees seem to have done best, their pay rising from an average £9,300 in 1979 to £16,500 in 1988. The average for those concerns now privatized rose from £8,257 in 1979 to £13,800 in 1988. Those still in the public sector saw their pay go up from £9,060 in 1979 to £11,920 in 1988.

The figures for those at the top, of course, included performance-related pay, which, for most, did not exist when their organizations were nationalized. But they do not include significantly increased perks, pension rights and, where necessary, redundancy payments. When Sir Gordon Dunlop, finance director of British Airways, left the company by mutual agreement (which followed a mutual disagreement) he was paid a total of £895,000, including pension rights and £511,000 compensation for loss of office.

But if these figures seem large, they pale beside the fees and commission paid to professional advisers, public relations firms and advertising agencies. There is no doubt that privatization helped the City of London through a lean time following Big Bang, while those advertising and public relations agencies that did not share in the Government spoils were put at a singular disadvantage.

In the first decade of privatization, the Government spent about £120 million on advertising, providing a very valuable boost to the national Press and television, and, of course, to the select number of advertising agencies it used. By 1990, Collett Dickenson & Pearce had emerged as the most favoured advertising agency, but this was largely due to the huge spend on water privatization, which cost almost as much as the first 12 sell-offs. Young & Rubican handled about £33 million worth of advertising for British Gas, in what was an unusual and controversial compaign featuring the mysterious Sid. This, in turn, dwarfed the British Telecom campaign worth £12.4 million, which had accounted for more than half the privatization spend in the first six years. Later, Valin Pollen was to handle British Airways, National Power and PowerGen, while Charles Barker looked after the British Airports Authority.

Just how these agencies, and the other privileged few, were picked has been the subject of intensive argument in the advertising industry. Generally, a handful of shops were short-listed from the list of agencies who had satisfied the Whitehall publicity machines and the Central Office of Information that they were capable of the job. Those fortunate enough to have got on a short-list had nearly always been asked to come up with their final pitch in under a fortnight, and that pitch was not to ministers but to others charged with executing the particular sell-off, including, much to the agencies' irritation and disquiet, the public relations people.

Generally, those on the short-list had to be full-service agencies with experience of working on a major Government campaign or handling a flotation for a major international corporation. The Government decided it could not risk awarding a privatization float to a smaller niche agency.

King of the PR groups has undoubtedly been Dewe Rogerson, a City of London firm that has been much favoured by the Thatcher Government against other publicists.

Dewe Rogerson, named after its founders Roddy Dewe and Nick Rogerson, was one of the fathers of the modern financial public relations industry. Until it came along, financial PR consisted of sending out dusty and dull hand-outs containing company annual results to the City editors of the national and regional Press. 'It coincided with the first columns about finance in anything other than the pink paper,' said Mark Carlisle, the firm's managing director, though to be strictly accurate newspapers like *The Times* had City columns and coverage long before the 60s.

Dewe Rogerson brought a certain style to corporate and financial relations that was previously evident only in product sales; but the firm only came into real prominence on the back of the privatizations.

The skilful financial public relations consultant is adept at drawing the investing public's attention to new issues, working to make sure that investment analysts, financial institutions and the financial media are well informed about the more positive aspects of the company being floated. Financial PR people are also particularly active in mergers and acquisitions; it is by no means unusual for senior consultants called in to help fight a hostile takeover to draw fees equivalent to those of corporate lawyers or merchant bankers.

The British Telecom campaign was the first, and it was directed at the general public. 'It was plain that there was insufficient appetite in the City for the shares,' said Carlisle later. 'It was entirely improbable that there would be sufficient appetite from overseas. And the secret of a share offering is to create a perception of scarcity.'

The campaign worked, and Dewe Rogerson then won the account for privatizing Britoil, British Gas, the Trustee Savings Bank, BP, British Steel, and the water and electricity industries. This business helped it to achieve the Number 20 spot in the *Campaign* 300, with billings in 1988 of £73 million.

There have been many who have questioned the wisdom of allocating so much power and influence to one City firm: indeed, when the time came to pitch for the electricity account only Lowe Bell, headed by Tim Bell, one of Mrs Thatcher's recent image advisers, sought to challenge Dewe Rogerson's dominance. Other large agencies decided that once the Prime Minister had over-ruled her former Energy Secretary, Cecil Parkinson – who had recommended a variety of agencies be asked to sell the distribution and generating companies of England and Wales – the die was cast. They were right.

The force behind Dewe Rogerson is Mark Carlisle, a City-type in his 40s, of pre-yuppie mould, educated at Charterhouse and Sussex University, who has somehow managed to diminish his undoubted effectiveness behind a veneer of arrogance that has won him few friends amongst media people. I suspect the dislike some felt for him, partly because of the privileged position his company has held, coloured their judgement, for it became only too clear that the almost universally expressed view of the serious newspapers – that the water privatization campaign was unpopular with the public – was totally wrong. Sid's thirst for water was unquenched.

Dewe Rogerson's remit was not confined to public relations: it was also handed the job of selecting advertising agencies for the £20-million splurge on advertisements for the water sell-off. This infuriated many agency heads who believed it ethically questionable that Carlisle should help to judge an agency's ability while still in competition with them.

The trade publication *Campaign*, reporting the views of the industry, found several agency bosses ever ready with the ribald quote. 'He is a slimy individual who wouldn't know a good ad if it bit him on the bum,' said one vitriolic non-admirer.

Carlisle manages to shrug off this kind of abuse with more sorrow than anger, saying he sees his job as getting the work done which best reflects the strategy for the client rather than complacently accepting everything put in front of him. He also pointed out that he was not the final arbiter in the decision to appoint agencies, but only an important part of the process.

Dewe Rogerson, in many privatizations, also had to play a part in ensuring that government publicity guidelines were upheld, even though ultimate control lay with the civil servants. These guidelines were wide and various, and the critical observer may view the interpretation of some of them with a cynical eye.

The civil servants at the Treasury's office in Great George Street were on the look out for any waste of money. 'Is it necessary, is it affordable?', they asked. 'Can the results be measured? Is the campaign the most economical, efficient and effective?' One only has to read these questions to imagine that Treasury mandarins may not be the best judges of a creative campaign. They needed someone like Mark Carlisle or Roddy Dewe to tell them.

Then there were issues of propriety, monitored by the Cabinet Office. They had to be sure that any advertising campaign was relevant to government responsibilities. They stipulated – though with what degree of insistence I know not – that advertisements should be objective and explanatory, not tendentious or polemical. They demanded, though often perhaps did not get, a justification for the expenditure of public funds. And they said that campaigns should not be party political.

Other restrictions which those involved in the campaigns had to watch were restraints imposed by the Companies Act and the 1988 Financial Services Act. The latter was deemed by lawyers to be the most onerous, and led to many a heated late-night squabble. Under the Financial Services Act, all prospectus advertising has to be approved by an 'authorized person', and cleared by the Securities and Investments Board, or one of its attached self-regulatory organizations, such as the International Stock Exchange of London. Advertisements had to carry a disclaimer on the likelihood of an investment decreasing in value.

Legal advisers – and public relations men when it suited them – sought refuge behind the Financial Services Act to advise company chairmen and finance directors to refuse to appear on radio and television programmes to answer tough questions. It took a long argument with Dewe Rogerson before I was able to talk to Sir Denis Rooke about the privatization of British Gas for a Channel Four programme. Lawyers did their best to prevent me from having an interview with Lord King of Wartnaby in the run-up to the British Airways float. In the end, both chairmen seemed pleased to talk, and were frank and open, but their adviser hovered around anxiously. What made their concerns – and the regulations – ridiculous was that the merchant bankers and others invoking these rules flouted the regulations themselves by giving financial journalists on the Sunday newspapers long 'exclusive' unattributable interviews. In many of these, they blatantly made information available which was both against the spirit and the letter of the regulations.

In any event, someone in Dewe Rogerson must have known a good advertisement when they saw it, because the water campaign, using an H_2O logo on a letter as a franking device, providing a watermark effect, quickly achieved its objective: public awareness of water businesses which previously had only been thought of as dull utilities run by equally dull people. Water was also promoted as an environmentally good investment: sensible at a time when 'green' ways of saving were gaining fashion.

As *Campaign* writer Vicki Scott explained, persuading the public to buy shares in privatization schemes requires more than ham-fisted promotion: the public need intelligent publicity material.

With all large 'offers for sale' the aim is to encourage as many people as possible to subscribe for shares, yet a large proportion of the market is unaware of the company's

breadth and performance. In addition to reaching, inform-
ing and creating interest in a target market, the other main
objective is to achieve the best possible share price by
creating an impression of scarcity.

In the light of current economic pressure and the controversial standing of certain 'offers for sale', it is clear the
communications strategies adopted will have a delicate and
vital role to play if sufficient investors and a good share
price are to be attracted.

Ms Scott is right about the vital role of communications, but
whether the campaigns created by Dewe Rogerson deserve the
description 'delicate' is questionable. 'Cynical' and 'slanted'
seem to me to be more appropriate adjectives. Until privatization, no one thought it necessary to advertise water or the water
authorities: what Dewe Rogerson did was to orchestrate the
pretence that the thousands of pages of advertising that sustained the newspapers and television stations during the
Summer of 1989 had somehow been the upshot of a campaign
dreamed up by the mandarins that ran the water industry,
rather than a government-funded effort to heighten awareness.

But that was its job, and it did it well, certainly heightening
awareness, and in a very short space of time, no mean feat in
itself. As for the agencies who participated, they loved the
privatization campaigns, not so much because it was a gravy
train, but because many of them were works of creative art that
people remembered. The downside was that they required a
huge pool of resources, including extra staff who often had to be
laid off at the end of the work.

At least the activities of the PR people were reasonably
visible, which is more than can be said of the other advisers –
solicitors, accountants, merchant bankers and stockbrokers. All
these groups had conducted their activities with an excessive
degree of secrecy, and only a few of those involved have been
prepared to discuss their role openly, concealing information
under the traditional British cloak of the need for secrecy.

In the case of the merchant bankers and stockbrokers, their
reluctance to be open is all the more to be regretted given their

penchant to talk their heads off, particularly to analysts and the media, about private flotations. In such floats there had also been some account taken of consumer interests, whereas the only representation of the consumer at privatization discussions had been undertaken by ministers. As Matthew Bishop and John Kay of the London Business School said in their report, *Does Privatization Work?*:

> Senior management interests, by contrast, are represented very strongly indeed. Employees of the concern to be privatized play no part at all in the process. It cannot be said that the public statements by their representatives suggest that this role would be a constructive one, but exclusion aggravates this – it is easier to be irresponsible if you have no responsibility. Very little of the expensively purchased advice and analysis is available to Parliament in its legislative scrutiny of the proposals.

The professional advisers were also reluctant to discuss their fees, either as an hourly rate or as a total cost. One would have to ferret through the records of the National Audit Office to get some kind of measure of the huge fees, commissions and promotional spending handed out by the Government. There is no doubt that the Conservative Government has rewarded its friends in the City very generously indeed.

Consider the privatization of British Gas. It cost £159 million – or 3 per cent of the total amount raised. Put in simple terms, that is twice the percentage amount paid to an estate agent for the sale of an average house, which many people already believe excessive.

Of the £159 million, by far the largest amount, £60 million or 37 per cent, was used for underwriting and broking. Yet British Gas was heavily over-subscribed, and an extremely low-risk operation for the underwriters. By contrast, the underwriting and broking costs for British Airways were, at £7.8 million, only 27 per cent of the total costs, and the risks, and international content, of the underwriting were significantly greater.

Some privatizations appear to have been particularly expensive operations – for no good reason. The £1.28 billion sale of the British Airports Authority is a good example of unnecessary extravagance. Underwriting costs at £13.6 million were 31 per cent, and very high for the sale of an asset backed by property as desirable as London's Heathrow and Gatwick Airports. The public relations and advertising bills were well over the top at £10 million: it cost almost £4 million more to sell the BAA than British Airways, and £6 million more than Rolls-Royce. As a result of this lavish spending of public money, the BAA float was the most costly of all the major privatizations. The taxpayer was charged expenses of 7.4 per cent of the revenue raised, compared with 4.4 per cent in the case of British Gas, 4.7 per cent in the case of British Airways, and 2.2 per cent in the case of Rolls-Royce. So far as I am aware, no one has been asked to account publicly for this largesse and excessive generosity to professional advisers.

The other middlemen who have made excessive profits from privatization are, of course, the institutions – big life assurance and unit trust companies, and pension funds. In so far as this may be of benefit to those whose investments and pensions are cared for by these bodies – and that means most of us – this may not be quite as undesirable as it sounds.

Perhaps it is being unnecessarily prudish to suggest that the income and growth of the funds should be the result of sound investment judgement and the work ethic rather than clever speculation. After all, we all like a flutter from time to time. But I cannot believe that it is either rational or desirable that privatization should allow these institutions to act as middlemen and make very large short-term speculative gains – simply because the Government has often found it difficult to get its pricing of privatization issues right.

Let me explain this. When it has come to pricing privatization issues, the Government has sought the advice of the major investment institutions. Understandably, they have pitched the figure at the lowest level they believe does not strain credibility. Since overseas institutions have been permitted only a limited stake in privatization issues, the institutions have been able to get away with this. So when British Telecom, British Gas and British Airways came to the market, the very institutions that talked down the stock, who said that gas prices might weaken, or that BA was a high-risk business, sold parts of their allocations overnight to overseas buyers. The premium on British Telecom was over 80 per cent, that on the Trustee Savings Bank and British Airways over 50 per cent, on Amersham International over 30 per cent, and British Gas 20 per cent.

In these cases – and in a number of others – the Government appears to have misjudged the market. Or, to put it in a less charitable way, it was conned by the City into believing that the equity in privatization issues would not be over-subscribed and would be worth less than proved to be the case. It is easy to be wise after the event, of course, and even in these days of barely credible politicians, it is probably too cynical to believe that the Thatcher Government priced the issues at bargain-basement levels in order to curry favour with the electorate. Each issue could have been priced at 15 per cent more, and still have been highly popular. I prefer the conspiracy theory: that the City, ever ready to look short-term, saw the opportunity of making a quick buck, and seized it.

This, of course, is extremely undesirable: even if you are a beneficiary of one of these investment institutions, it is morally wrong. The indications are that the Government itself believes it has been taken for a ride – and as it gets more experienced in privatizations is less likely to be conned. When he was Chancellor of the Exchequer, Nigel Lawson increased the pressure on the City to underwrite privatization issues at substantially lower margins than had been the case with British Telecom and British Gas.

There is a solution – or several solutions. One would be to release only 10 per cent of an issue at a time. The Japanese government did this very successfully with the world's biggest float – that of Nippon Telephone and Telegraph (NTT). Another would be to sell at a fixed price only to individuals – and to have the institutions tender for their stock.

· 12 ·

The billion-dollar business

UNDOUBTEDLY THE BEST rewarded – and least deserving – of the professionals involved in the privatization business have been the underwriters: securities houses, merchant banks and clearing banks, most of them British, who guaranteed that all the shares on offer would be sold on pain of having to buy and hold them themselves should any issue flop.

With popular government issues there is virtually no risk. The professional underwriter knows that the shares on offer will always be priced to attract the small investor, and that the issue will therefore be over-subscribed. Underwriters also know that a large number of investment institutions, both from Britain and overseas, will want to have a substantial slice of any privatized industry in their portfolio. There are now more than a dozen privatized companies in the FT-100 Share Index, so those fund managers who believe in the new craze of indexation – building a portfolio which mirror images any given index – would have to acquire their share of any new offer.

So far as I can discover, only once have underwriters been really caught out, and that was in the final sell-off of the British Government's stake in British Petroleum, when the great stock-market crash of October 1987 forced market prices well below the offer price. Even then the underwriters were partly bailed out by the Kuwait Investment Office, which picked up a good part of the shares, and were then forced, ignominiously, to sell them again by Lord Young, the Secretary for Trade and Industry.

The BP case provides a good example of underwriting in action, as it is supposed to work, and it is to the credit of the Government, and Mrs Thatcher in particular, that it lent a deaf ear to the yelps of protest from the City demanding the issue be postponed. For once the underwriters were taking a caning, and they didn't like it.

· 13 ·

Privatization and the punter

SHARE CLUBS HAVE been springing up all over the country,
the enthusiasm for investment on the sharemarkets having been
fostered by privatization. The clubs are classless: there is no
evidence at all that they are the preserve of the middle classes.
The price of shares in British Gas is just as likely to be discussed
on the production line at a baked bean factory as in a drawing-
room.

I once came upon just such a conversation in the Conservative Club at West Houghton, a small and unpretentious village
in the industrial belt between Liverpool and Manchester. 'I
am hanging on to my British Telecom,' said one woman,
'because everyone is installing fax machines and I think they
will benefit.'

How did she keep an eye on shares? 'I watch the prices every
morning in the *Daily Mail*,' she said, 'and sometimes I keep a
watch on them through teletext on the telly.' In other words,

she was not doing much different from the average professional investor, and applying sound logic and common sense to her investment decisions.

It is the Thatcher Government – and not the City of London – that one has to thank for such examples of popular capitalism. Even before the giant shake-up in the financial markets created by Big Bang in 1987, the City had displayed a kind of mean contempt for private individuals with less than £50,000 to invest (in other words, for all but a very minor proportion of the populace).

But until the British Telecom float, with its hype, touring road shows, television campaign and gimmicks like bonus shares and vouchers to help pay the phone bills, only about two million Britons, or just over 3 per cent of the population, owned shares. One year later, that figure had increased to 8 per cent ... etcetera, etcetera.

However, not everyone held on to their shares. Many of them traded them in, and opted for other privatizations, rather than increase their overall holdings. By the time British Telecom had produced its first annual report as a privatized company, the number of individual investors had fallen from 2.3 million to 1.5 million. A year later the figure was slightly less.

The inducements offered by the Government to persuade shareholders to stay in were substantial, but did not appear to work. They included discounts on future telephone bills, and a free issue of extra shares for those who maintained their holding for three years. But many decided to take their profit, and wait for the next privatization.

The perks with British Gas turned out to be more generous, and Rothschild, the merchant bank advising the Government, wisely counselled that each gas customer should be guaranteed an allocation of £250 worth of shares. Letters went out from Sir Denis Rooke, the chairman of British Gas, to more than 16 million households, the largest direct-mail campaign ever launched in Britain. He told them that if they registered as customers, they would get preferential treatment over other applicants, and that if they kept their stake for more than three years, they would be able to claim one bonus share for every ten purchased, or £10 vouchers to set against their gas bills at the rate of one for every 100 shares bought, subject to an upper limit.

I suspect the reason the public has fallen for privatization is, indeed, because of the clever mass-marketing used by both the Government and the corporations being floated. The Government has been at a great advantage in selling off nationalized industries: it has been able to sequestrate huge chunks of public money for some of the marketing campaigns, as well as adding its official endorsement to the product. It has also brazenly broken the rules laid down by the Stock Exchange for major flotations.

The public has also been penalized, compared with the institutions, in privatization issues, although things have improved somewhat since the débâcle when the Government sold its remaining 49 per cent stake in its North Sea oil company, Britoil, in the mid-80s. Only 15 per cent of the issue was reserved for the ordinary public, off-loading most of the rest to the institutions, both City and overseas. The Japanese, in particular, could not believe their luck, for with the yen strengthening against a falling pound, they had a bargain.

While the Japanese cashed in, the miserly amount reserved for the British public was over-subscribed ten times. Those applying for between 200 and 1,100 shares were allocated only 100; those seeking between 1,200 and 1,400 got 150; and those optimistic enough to seek more than 1,400 were awarded none at all. Why the more enthusiastic British investor should be so unfairly penalized is beyond belief, given the generosity shown by the Government's adviser, Lazards, towards Japanese pension funds and Swiss banks. 'We were conned,' said a letter writer to the *Financial Times*. 'What a fiasco,' wrote another.

Small shareholders, many of them Conservative voters so assiduously fostered by the Government, were left with holdings which were about as useful as a clutch of premium bonds. As I commented at the time:

What real use were 100 partly-paid up shares? Bought for £100, they had, after listing, a market value of about £120.

Those who wanted to take a profit could not follow the Japanese life assurance companies and sell out. The £20 profit turned out to be worthless once the minimum £15 commission and VAT had been paid. And when allowance had been made for the amounts paid on cheques submitted with application forms and held by those handling the sale for an unconscionable time, those selling would have made a loss. And investors deciding to hang on to the shares were left with a piffling long-term investment.

· 14 ·

What about the workers?

THE SERVICE IS better on British Airways these days, and if we are to believe a documentary on BBC Television in early 1990, it is because every employee has been on a one-day training course to learn how to 'put people first'.

Undoubtedly such courses, however brief, do help to motivate staff, but I prefer to believe that the principal catalyst for change is that large numbers of British Airways employees – particularly flight attendants who know a bargain when they see one – have been able to increase their assets and pocket some useful dividends by owning shares in the airline. And, as employees, they were able to buy shares when British Airways was privatized on especially advantageous terms.

Nearly all employees of privatized concerns in Britain have fared well as a result of taking a stake in the company. Let us look at another example: the employees of Northumbrian Water, the most over-subscribed of the ten new water companies.

Those who did not live in Northumbria were restricted to just 100 shares each, and even the customers were allocated only 200: hardly worth the bother, and almost a waste of time. Those who worked for the company, however, had every reason to smile, for they were entitled to apply for and get up to 5,000 shares. Workers at the other companies received the same preferential treatment.

The Northumbrian shares were priced at £2.40, payable in

instalments, but water employees were able to invest at a 10 per cent discount. When trading started on the sharemarkets, the opening price showed a premium of 60 pence a share. A worker taking his full allocation would have shown a paper profit of about £3,000.

The water workers – along with other employees of privatized concerns – also enjoyed other special privileges denied to others, the most significant of which was exemption from the punitive taxation imposed on their counterparts who worked for other companies seeking extra capital through rights issues. Although companies offering rights issues normally allocate shares to employees – through the distribution of the so-called 'pink forms' signifying a priority offer – those workers who take advantage of this have to pay tax as PAYE on the premium to the issue price when the share starts trading, as if it was income. Indeed, so unfair is this rule that most employees end up having this tax deducted from their wages before they are able to dispose of the shares. The workers of privatized companies faced no such intolerable burden.

The 90,000 workers of British Gas were given generous treatment, which cost the taxpayer a total of £54 million. Each employee was awarded £70 worth of shares, plus a further £2 worth for each year of service. Those able to invest their own money were given two free shares for each one bought, up to a limit of £300 of free shares. Those inclined to dig deeper into their savings could buy up to £2,000 worth at a 10 per cent discount. Retired British Gas employees were also each given about £70 worth of free shares. This was in sharp contrast to the parsimony of British Telecom, whose shareholders missed out.

Apart from share ownership, privatized companies have introduced substantial profit-sharing schemes. In the first year of its scheme, British Telecom paid out £18 million in shares to its 230,000 employees. Payments, which were related to grades, varied from £80 for the lowest to £180 at the top.

One reason why the Government wanted employees to get preferential treatment in both launch share issues and in profit allocations was because it believed that if the workers were partners in an enterprise, they would be more acquiescent in labour relations, and less likely to demand high pay and go on strike for it. This does not appear to have worked. As evidenced elsewhere in this book, senior managers and directors have been especially generous in rewarding themselves, while the unions have not hesitated to push their demands to the full.

Although 85 per cent of employees were shareholders, this did not stop British Telecom workers from striking in the Winter of 1987 – just when demand for new services was at its peak. Two years after privatization, British Telecom was turning in profits of over £1 billion, an 11 per cent increase over the previous year, had cut its workforce by 5,000, and raised output per employee from £28,100 to £35,900. The 110,000 engineers were not too impressed with the offer of a 5 per cent pay-rise, and called the first ever all-out stoppage.

John Golding, general secretary of the National Communications Union, blamed privatization for leading British Telecom executives to attempt to introduce a hard-nosed corporate culture, and compared, rather disingeniously, the old British Telecom with sound Japanese industrial practice:

We had lifetime employment, commitment to serving the customers with high quality, combined with internal flexibility. Now BT seems to be taking an approach similar to GEC's? Why on earth do they want to make us similar to British manufacturing industry?

After an acrimonious two weeks, a two-year pay and productivity deal worth 12.75 per cent was struck, while BT dropped some of the efficiency demands it had set its heart on. At the end of the financial year – despite an increase in profits, up 11 per cent to £2.07 billion – BT refused to pay out profit-sharing payments to its workers, whether they were involved in the industrial action or not. The then chairman, Sir George Jefferson, said that although the strike had had a neutral effect on profits, it would have been 'very difficult for customers to understand us supporting a continuation of the scheme this year'. Golding retorted that the decision was 'petty-minded, vindictive and short-sighted'.

In all the major privatizations so far, the majority of employees have taken up their entitlements, though many later sold or reduced their shares. Foolishly perhaps, most employees sold their holdings on the market, rather than to work colleagues or trades unions, for had they adopted this latter course they could have wielded more influence in their companies. This happened, to some extent, in the case of British Airways, where 5,000 employees gave their union a proxy vote over their shares.

Since the BT days, many unions have decided to take a more pragmatic line towards share ownership. For example, the eight unions in the Electricity Supply Trades Union Council claim that they are still vehemently opposed to privatization of Britain's power industry, but in early 1990 were accepting that they could do little to stop it and were hard at work trying to negotiate a more generous hand-out. As John Lyons, general secretary of the Engineers' and Managers' Association, put it: 'We have to deal with practicalities. Members will be given shares, and it is our job to get them the best deal possible.' Another trades unionist, Jim Mowatt, of the leftish Transport and General Workers' Union, added: 'People do have ideological objections, but you have to confront reality, and the reality is that workers want shares.'

This kind of statement would have been inconceivable at the start of the great privatizations. Now the goal of many union leaders is to secure 10 per cent or more of the voting stock of companies for workers. They are also increasing their interest in ESOPS (Employee Share Ownership Plans), whereby trusts are set up within companies to enable money to be borrowed to buy shares to be distributed to workers at a later date. The money is later repaid by the trust out of company profits. The Government strongly supports this concept, although it has gathered ground more slowly than might otherwise be the case because its merits have not been publicized adequately.

· 15 ·
The grey market

'Don't get mad: get even'
– President George Bush

WHEN YOU DEAL in favourites, those denied equality of
opportunity normally seek other means to achieve their goals.
By giving the City and big British investment institutions
preferential treatment in privatization issues, government ministers ensured that those rich or powerful or astute enough to do
so would find ways whereby they could get even.

In times of war or deprivation, black markets are created. In
the Soviet Union under Brezhnev, there was widespread racke-
tering in goods that could normally only be sold to foreigners in
special shops. In these shops, the windows were all blacked out
so that the ordinary Russian could not see either who was
shopping or what they were buying. That did not stop Soviet
traders from buying these goods and selling them on at a profit.
When Britain had exchange controls limiting the amount of
spending money a family could take for a fortnight's holiday on
the Spanish Costas, there was no limit to the spending of those
wealthy enough to have an American Express card. American
servicemen on British bases were able to buy goods at special
rates on station; some of them then sold them on to local traders.

In the case of privatization, many of those who knew they

would get shares in government issues disposed of them before trading began, in what became known as the 'grey market'. These sellers, many of them well-known financial institutions, were the equivalent of ticket touts at Wembley or Wimbledon, except that they spoke with polished accents. Like football or tennis fans, the buyers were desperate to buy, having been denied access to the issue through normal means. And, like the Football Association or the All England Lawn Tennis Club, the Government frowned on the practice, but tolerated it.

Realistically the Government had no choice, because it created the conditions that led to the establishment of the grey market in privatization issues. Take the case of British Gas. Forty per cent of the allocation was designated for the British public. A smaller percentage went to British institutions. A 20 per cent parcel of shares was allocated to overseas investors. If the issue was over-subscribed (inevitable, unless the advertising campaign was a total flop), then almost half of this would be clawed back and allocated to the public.

Applications closed on Friday 5 December 1986. The following Monday afternoon, 8 December, trading in British Gas would open on the London Stock Exchange. But private individuals would trade at their own risk, because they would not know how many shares they had been allocated until a week later, on 15 December. The institutions would have a field day, because the overseas investors, denied access to British Gas, would come in and buy stock from them at a premium the moment trading began.

Rather in the manner that a bookmaker creates odds before a horse race, many people in the markets began making judgements on the price at which British Gas shares would open when official trading began. Inevitably, this led to unofficial trading in advance, much of it directly between those who knew each other well enough to do so. But there were many who felt that if they could get a premium price before the float, this would provide a useful capital gain. Many others, most of them large companies and institutions in Europe, felt that by agreeing to buy British Gas shares before the float, they at least knew the premium; by waiting until after, they might end up paying more. Their judgement was correct. The grey market was what brought these two forces together.

Rather surprisingly, the London Stock Exchange banned its members from participating in the grey market in British Gas shares, thereby denying stockbrokers some useful commission. They could not ban the market itself, nor could they stop institutions from by-passing the Stock Exchange altogether, which many of them did. But the Exchange rightly pointed out that if it gave trading in the grey market its official blessing, then private individuals might be tempted to sell the shares they thought they would receive before they were allocated them. And, if allocations were lower than expected, they would then be selling holdings they did not own. This practice, known as 'short-selling', is widely practised by institutions, but discouraged for individuals, for obvious reasons.

Ian Salter, chairman of the Quotations Committee, told me:

> The main reason, really, is that until the certainty of the issue is known to our members, it would be allowing them to deal in a situation (a) in which they do not know whether the issue will go ahead, or (b) if their clients are going to get an allocation of shares.

I went in search of the grey market, expecting to find those practising it to be operating inconspicuously behind locked doors on the first floor of a 1930s shopping precinct in an outer-suburb like Enfield or Streatham, or in the back room of a semi-detached on the Bath Road near Heathrow, where, years before, we had discovered a dealer called Khemlani raising money from Iraq to finance the Australian spending spree of the Whitlam government. But I had allowed my imagination to run rout. One phone call, a friendly telephonist, and a cordial invitation from her boss to visit the premises and see the dealing room in operation, took me just a few steps from Liverpool Street station in the heart of the City to perhaps the liveliest, and only, trading room in British Gas shares in London.

My visit took place five days before official trading began, two days before the issue closed to the public. There was nothing secretive or improper about this grey market operation, and its proprietor, a licensed securities dealer but not a member of the Stock Exchange, took pains to explain to me that, for his own protection against bad risk and bad debt, his firm only dealt with blue chip institutions who could be relied upon to settle their bills. A blackboard the length of the dealing room denoted transactions, marking the price at which British Gas shares were changing hands, and the institutions, British and overseas, who were trading them. I was allowed to photograph the room and the trading price, then 63 pence, but asked not to identify the customers without their permission. The dealers behaved much as would those in any City dealing room, except that these seemed older, wiser and more experienced.

While I was there, the leading French institution, Banque Indo-Suez, purchased 100,000 non-existent British Gas shares for the 63 pence asking price. I later visited their offices, where their London fund manager, Martin Mathanson, saw no reason to be secretive and was very frank as to why he had used the grey market. He said:

> Most of the institutions and players in the City are participants. At times like this when you have a share issue of great importance, it is not always possible for people on the Continent to get a good piece of the action, simply because most of it is being earmarked for the man in the street in England. So these people have to look at the grey market because otherwise they may not get the stock they require.

At the grey market dealing room I visited, members of the public were discouraged, unless they were buyers and paid cash. The proprietor had rightly decided he could not risk allowing them to sell their future shares to him in case they did not get any.

So, while the grey markets clearly serve some purpose, they are of little help to the man in the street, who has to wait for at least one week after the big institutions before trading. Paul

Manduca, an accountant with Touche Ross, and a stern critic of the grey markets, still felt sorry for the private shareholder:

> In the interests of wider share ownership, I think it is disappointing that people will not have their allotment letters on the first day of official dealings. I think it is because of that that there is something of a false market in the first week, and as institutions clamber to build up their weightings, private shareholders will not be able to deal until their allotment letters are in their hands.
>
> I have not yet been able to get a satisfactory explanation as to why private individuals should be put at a disadvantage to institutions. To put it another way, I see no reason why the Thatcher Government should not have been able to find a way to practise what it preaches – and to put people before special interest groups. In these days of highly computerized records, it should be possible to issue shares to the public before official trading begins.

· 16 ·

A nice little monopoly

'After bats, pike and fine-leaved hemlock water dropworts, why should it surprise me that there are roe-deer living within 400 yards of the runway?'
– Naturalist Gerald Durrell, on Gatwick Airport, in an advertisement for the British Airports Authority

'If the London airports were separated, they would be killed by the Paris and Amsterdam airports. The French, Germans and Dutch would be popping the champagne bottles'
– Sir Norman Payne, chairman of the British Airports Authority

AIRPORTS REFLECT THE countries in which they are located. Changi Airport in Singapore is a model of efficiency and sound planning: externally it is concrete and functional, but inside it has tasteful design and decor. Charles de Gaulle at Roissy near Paris is full of Gallic eccentricity: there is no mistaking you are in France. Schipol Amsterdam is neat and tidy, with stalls selling tulip bulbs, Delft pottery and Gouda cheeses.

And Britain's Heathrow and Gatwick Airports are like those shopping malls that sprout up in provincial towns, befitting the tastes of the nation of shopkeepers.

This makes some people very angry. 'The British Airports Authority is more interested in the shopping public than getting the bloody planes out on time,' one harassed British Airways executive told me. 'The congestion here is bad enough with the number of passengers, let alone all the shoppers.'

It is perhaps inevitable that there should be tension between airline operators and airport owners, but the BA man had a point. Whereas most airports are limited to a news-stand, a gift shop, and duty free shops on the air-side of customs and immigration, the terminals at London's Heathrow are like a galleria, with branches of the Sock Shop, Tie Rack and Shirt Shop, and large supermarkets where you can buy anything from wine gums to waistcoats, and from Beefeater dishclothes to designer leather. Gatwick is even worse: there is a whole floor devoted to shopping and fast-food, and as you mingle in the crowd it is hard to imagine that you are in an airport at all. It is not surprising that many passengers fail to get to the departure gates on time.

Most of this is the consequence of privatization. The directors of the BAA seem to get much more joy from the tinkling of the cash registers on the shopping parades than from the prompt departure of a flight. At Gatwick, when tens of thousands of Britons annually spend the duration of a working day waiting for the inevitably delayed holiday flight, the holders of the retail and catering franchises rub their hands with glee.

Freed from the restrictions of being a department of government, the BAA has also entered the market itself. Not content with simply collecting the ever-rising franchise fees, it has formed a subsidiary and opened a shop called 'Teddys', selling soft toys in Gatwick's new North Terminal. Sir Norman Payne, BAA's chairman, seems to have ambitions in retailing beyond airports. He has signed a contract with the area health authority in Cambridge to develop 'retail facilities' at Addenbrook's Hospital, so that those who have no immediate hope of flying can at least imagine they are at Stansted and enjoy the doubtful and expensive benefits of airport shopping. The BAA also has an interest in Downtown, a duty free shop to be located in Central London enabling travellers to select goods prior to departure. One can only imagine the congestion when rich foreign travellers turn up at the departure gate to collect their spoils, and try to push their way on to the planes with their 'hand luggage'.

Of BAA's total revenue of £523 million in the 1987–88 year, less than half (43.6 per cent) was accounted for by activities which directly relate to the flying business. The lion's share (53.9 per cent) came from duty free shops and other retailing, and from other activities like car-parking. Now that the BAA is trying to squeeze a profit from every corner, it can cost more to park a car at Heathrow and Gatwick than in London's West End or City. Such is the disadvantage of having a government only too ready to hand out a private monopoly.

Curiously there is nothing in BAA's mission statement, published post-privatization, to suggest it has retailing ambitions. The mission statement says:

We aim to achieve a consistent growth in earnings per share and in the return on net assets employed which puts our performance amongst the highest of the 100 largest quoted companies in the United Kingdom.

We will give safety and security the highest priority at all our airports.

We aim to remain the world's leading international airport group and intend to be recognized as such.

We will keep our shareholders well informed about the development of the business.

We will deal with customers, shareholders, staff, suppliers and other business partners with the utmost integrity.

We will constantly seek to improve the service we provide to our customers, including passengers, airlines and other airport users.

We will strive to have an efficient, well-motivated and well-informed staff.

We will seek to be a good neighbour to the communities surrounding our airports.

Those who follow the business of the BAA would question whether some of these ambitions have seriously been attempted, let alone fulfilled. Certainly those who live within listening distance of the major airports would question whether the BAA is a good neighbour. It has paid scant attention to the limitations on night-time flying, and has been reluctant to discipline airlines that repeatedly flout the rules on flight-paths. It is perhaps too busy selling teddy bears.

But it has engaged in some extraordinary advertising campaigns, which appear to bear little relation to the business of running airports. Here is a privatized monopoly that has clearly run away with itself.

One double-page glossy colour spread, clearly designed to appeal to the greens among us, was headed, 'Flight EH 0203 from Gatwick', with the sub-title, 'The Little Owl, Athene noctus, hunts regularly over Gatwick's 2,400 acres of fields and woods'. The copy in the advertisment is attributed to naturalist Gerald Durrell, and we are invited to believe that he regularly goes on safari at the world's second busiest international airport, dodging the 747s and DC10s in order to spot blue Agrion damselflies carrying out aerobatic stunts. According to Durrell's copy, Gatwick is a 'happy hunting ground for grass snakes', 21 million people each year land and take off 'within 400 yards of a herd of wild roe-deer', while the man-made environmental banks screening the new North Terminal and housing its central-heating boilers are used by foxes as sun-beds. 'They also provide a fine larder of voles and field mice for the stoats, weasels and owls that live in the area.'

Durrell adds, in parenthesis: 'Little owls, plentiful in the Gatwick area, also carry leg-rings with numbers that sound like airline flights.'

In this flight of fancy there is no mention, needless to say, of shopping malls and departure delays, nor of the fact that Gatwick still has only one runway – used both by departing and landing aircraft – and creates a situation which is neither in the interests of safety nor good timekeeping.

One wonders whether this was what Mrs Thatcher and her ministers had in mind when the Government decided to hand over control of key airports to private interests. It also begs the question of what the Government will do when the Monopolies and Mergers Commission has carried out its five-year review, due to be completed in the Autumn of 1992.

The Government may well decide that the running of Britain's airports has become so eccentric that there is no need for the state to retain the golden share, thus making BAA vulnerable to takeover. No wonder ADT, the British industrial services group, with interests in the security business, was building up a stake in BAA in early 1990. If ever there was a privatized monopoly whose breakup would be in the national interest, it is BAA.

· 17 ·

Efficient monopolies?

'Telecommunications is a boom industry. It's going to be the most important growth industry of the next 25 years. We should look forward to the opportunities which will be opened to a privatized British Telecom, free to raise the money to do what it wants, free of control by politicians, bureaucrats and the Treasury'
– Kenneth Baker, Minister of Information Technology, and (later) chairman of the Conservative Party

'Any American living in Britain is understandably disgusted by the service provided by British Telecom'
– Philip Beresford, in the *Sunday Times*

WHEN, IN THE Spring of 1990, a group of local authorities in the Midlands region of Britain decided that they would club together and buy gas not from British Gas but from a private consortium, the press officer of the recently-privatized body reacted with utter dismay.

This for him, was not a perfect example of the free market working, or a determined attempt by some of the saner council officials to break the British Gas monopoly, but 'an attempt to disrupt a proven and established system'.

His comment, and the fact that it did not lead to a hue and

cry from either the popular or the serious Press, shows just how ready a resigned acceptance there has been in Britain of British Gas as a well-organized bully.

The British, alas, do not share the Americans' distaste of monopoly power, nor do their laws make significant provision against it. Perhaps if they did, the members of the Midlands local authorities at Birmingham, Coventry, Dudley, Sandwell, Solihull, Staffordshire, Walsall, Warwickshire and Wolver-hampton would have been given the credit they deserved for their foresight in saving the local population about £1 million in poll-tax bills.

The Midland Gas Consortium, as the group of authorities called themselves, had to go to considerable lengths to achieve the saving.

The Government has endowed British Gas with a monopoly on all domestic supplies, and has only opened it to competition on sites where the annual demand for gas exceeds more than 25,000 therms each year. What that means in real life is schools, sports and leisure centres and office blocks, where those who own or operate them, are free to find their gas from another source, although these suppliers still have no choice but to deliver it through British Gas pipelines. For most, this means the inconvenience is not worth the bother.

But the Midland Gas Consortium, which also included the West Midlands Police Authority, has, between its members, 630 sites using a total of about 35 million therms of gas a year, and was therefore able to wield substantial buying power. It went to Quadrant, a joint venture between two oil companies, Esso and Shell, and to Associated Gas Services, a company headed by Lord Ezra, formerly head of the National Coal Board. At the time of writing, it had not settled a contract with either of them, but had demonstrated beyond all doubt both that it could challenge the power of British Gas, but that to do so one almost has to have monopoly strength of one's own.

THE K-FACTOR

Where true competition with a privatized company does not exist, the Government has sought to control prices by a variety of means – the common principle being the so-called 'K-factor'. What this normally means is that prices may go up by the equivalent of the rise in the consumer price index, plus or minus a further percentage – which is determined by the appropriate government department – as being the amount needed for the organization to operate effectively.

In the case of British Gas, the K-factor was extra costs associated with the supply of gas from the North Sea fields becoming tighter and more expensive, less a percentage to take into account the degree by which Whitehall believes the corporation should become more efficient. At present the efficiency factor in the formula is 2 per cent.

This formula has been strongly critized by a one-time Thatcher Government adviser, Dr Irwin Stelzer, an American expert on utility regulation and managing director of the New York arm of Rothschilds. He told the *Financial Times*:

> If it doesn't allow adequate profits to be made, then you will know because the company will be unable to raise capital, but if profits are good after a few years, how will you know if they are monopoly profits or the result of efficiency? The interesting thing to me about the British approach to privatization is that no one thought through the regulatory consequences. The British fear of an excessively protracted, detailed regulatory system is leading them to a system in which the customer is essentially without recourse.

A new formula for British Gas pricing to household and commercial customers has to be in place by the Spring of 1992, and James McKinnon, the director-general of the Office of Gas Supply, the watchdog appointed by the Government to see over British Gas, has indicated that change is highly likely. He does not regard the present system as sacrosanct, and may call in the

Monopolies and Mergers Commission. Before he does that, he wants to conduct a root and branch examination of the industry's regime. Life will become tougher for British Gas, but whether it is as tough as true competition could provide is very debatable.

British Telecom is also a monopoly. When it was privatized, the Government would only allow one competitor to provide a private telephone service: Mercury, a subsidiary of Cable and Wireless, which was hardly a dynamic company. Mercury has proved more lively than its parent, and it has built up a business following in some major cities, but it has hardly touched the residential market, and it is unlikely to get more than 5 per cent of the overall market in the near future. Most people will have to put up with British Telecom.

ARE THEY MORE EFFICIENT?

But even if they are monopolies, are privatized public enterprises more efficient?

According to the London Business School study, *Does Privatization Work?* (1988), privatization has had little to do with promoting efficiency or improvements in productivity, and has brought no change to the levels of service provided by privatized companies. The study's authors, Matthew Bishop and John Kay, say that privatization is 'neither necessary nor sufficient' for changing companies' behaviour.

Bishop and Kay believe that economic benefits that are apparent to privatized industries do not appear to have resulted from the act of privatization itself. The greatest overall productivity improvements have taken place in British Steel, which has increased labour and capital productivity by 12.4 per cent on average since 1983. On the same basis, British Gas has improved by 6.2 per cent a year, British Coal by 4.6 per cent a year and British Telecom by only 2.5 per cent.

Other opinions vary, and there is plenty of evidence, both

scientific and anecdotal, to support a case either way. Judgement will have to be postponed for a few years yet, but the omens are not good for suggesting a notable increase in efficiency.

The longest experience, in Britain at least, is with British Telecom. Since its privatization, the volume of complaints from both business and the public has increased substantially.

In 1987, a study by Bryan Carlsberg, director-general of the Office of Telecommunications (OFTEL), set up by the Government as a watchdog on BT, produced a list of constant complaints: faults on customers' exchange lines and leased lines were taking longer than usual to repair; delays were increasing in the provision of new lines; and operator and directory enquiry services were unsatisfactory.

MPs on both sides of the House of Commons attacked BT's post-privatization record, while the campaigning group, Age Concern, published a report saying it was taking an unprecedented stand on the issue of privatization because 'of the effect it may have had on elderly and disabled patients'. Age Concern's report, published in July 1987, said:

> Since British Telecom was privatized in 1984, there has been widespread concern about the effect of its policies on poorer consumers, particularly elderly consumers. Elderly and disabled consumers have become worse off since privatization in virtually every aspect of telecommunication services.

The *Observer* newspaper reported how many of its readers had lost thousands of pounds worth of business because of BT inefficiencies, and failures to rectify faults. 'Success hangs frailly on our telephone bookings,' wrote a restaurateur in Pembroke, complaining that she had seen takings fall 60 per cent over a peak summer period because of indolence in repairing a line. Angus Hamilton from Dulwich in London phoned directory enquiries to get the number of OFTEL. 'I was told British Telecom had never heard of it,' he said.

One common complaint was that when telephones went dead,

nobody at BT seemed to want to do anything about it. Among those who complained to OFTEL was Joe Roeber, a London oil consultant. His phone kept ringing, but when he answered there was nobody there. 'BT's engineers did absolutely nothing,' he recalled. 'They came here, faffed about, and kept changing their story about what the problem was. They did not seem to have a system for tracing the fault.'

British Telecom's response to this was one of the favourite ploys of newly-privatized monopolies. It launched an advertising and public relations campaign. 'Is there a risk of British Telecom becoming popular?', lyricized the copy-writer in a rhetorical question in a £500,000 newspaper campaign. The Telecom Users' Association and the Telecom Managers' Association responded by pointing out that services were worsening, and that one in five phone boxes were out of order.

To be fair to British Telecom, not all of the problems were of its own making. One of the ironies was that at least part of BT's incompetence in dealing with complaints was due to a computer system it did not want imposed on it by the Conservative Government prior to privatization.

BT, with the help of the Logica computer consultancy, had devised Customer Service Systems (CSS), designed to handle the records of its millions of commercial and domestic customers, and to deal with billing, orders and complaints. Logica had created a similar system in Australia, and recommended that BT should use the powerful IBM 3081 mainframes in each of its 30 districts, where, typically, there are 700,000 telephone lines. The Tories vetoed this, insisting that the slower and incompatible British-made ICL computers be used in 12 of the districts. In the end only six ICLs were bought, because of delivery delays. Months later, and after BT had found it impossible to bill customers for most of a year in its Guildford district, the organization found it needed more powerful IBMs and ditched the ICLs – or, rather, relegated them to the accounts department. BT never admitted that its mistake was due to Government pressure, but at least it is a form of pressure which privatization has now removed.

Another irony is that anyone striving to start a new private business in the buoyant mid-Thatcher years was more likely to have their ambitions frustrated not by lack of finance or fiscal incentives, but by an inability to obtain telephone or fax lines. In 1987, I launched a new weekly newspaper for the *Financial Times* group, and we acquired modest offices in the Clerkenwell district of London near Smithfield market. We placed advertisements and recruited staff, signed typesetting and printing contracts, and were set to launch. Unfortunately British Telecom said it could not provide lines for six months.

You cannot run a newspaper without telephones. We entreated the local telephone manager to help us, but he said the delay was due to the non-arrival of imported equipment. We appealed to the army of British Telecom public relations officers without avail. Senior directors contacted BT directors. We did consider using portables as a temporary, if over-priced, expedient. In the end, and in desperation, I wrote to the Prime Minister at No 10, Downing Street. 'A new enterprise which will create at least 25 jobs is in jeopardy because of the failure of the newly-privatized British Telecom to provide essential telephone lines,' I wrote. 'Can you help?' Within a week we had our lines.

Three years later, we had much the same experience when we launched a new television programme requiring a microwave link from the *Financial Times* headquarters to the Telecom Tower in London's West End for onward transmission to the Cable News Network in the United States. First, British Telecom said it would take six months to arrange the link. After several complaints by us, BT reduced the time by half, arguing that the 'paperwork required' still meant the installation could not take place sooner. Finally, the job was completed in two months. In the United States, a similar arrangement can be executed in 24 hours.

A severe deterioration in BT's services since privatization is confirmed by Carlsberg in OFTEL's 1987–88 report:

For example, the success rate in repairing faults on private exchanges by the target time – the end of the working day after that in which the fault is reported – fell to about 74 per cent from the level of between 85 per cent and 90 per cent which had been emerging as the norm previously. Performance in providing new service deteriorated even more sharply.

It might have been hoped that this was a temporary aberration during the early days of the privatized British Telecom, and that as its rival, Mercury, became more drawn into the market the competition would force BT to become more efficient.

Mercury offers its customers a good service. Once a phone has been purchased, at a cost of about £75, there is a small rental in addition to the BT rental whose lines are used, but long-distance and international calls are significantly cheaper (for example, a three-minute peak-time call from London to New York presently costs £2.43; on Mercury, it's £1.98). Unfortunately, Mercury is not very good at publicizing itself, and by the start of the 90s, Mercury still had only 24,000 customers, compared with British Telecom's 22 million, while OFTEL's reports and criticisms became more strident. In 1989, OFTEL received 32,000 complaints about BT, a rise of over a third in a year, and in a period when profits rose sharply.

British Telecom itself was candid about the level of complaints, and put the volume at much higher than OFTEL, logging over one million protests a year. Among the most frequent and bizarre grumbles was the public's criticism of the BT complaints system itself by victims of what the company itself labelled 'Telecom shunt', the practice of transferring complainants from one department to another until they are finally cut off.

Not only is British Telecom inefficient: it also overcharges its customers, a classic phenomenon of an unchecked private monopoly. An international study of telephone charges by a firm of efficiency consultants, National Utility Services, found that Britain had become the most expensive country amongst the major industrial nations. A three minute local conversation in Britain cost 11 pence, compared with 5 pence in France, 5.8 pence in West Germany and 4.8 pence in the United States.

In the Spring of 1990, OFTEL was investigating this over-charging, believed by it to amount to more than £6 billion a year. Said Carlsberg:

> Britain should attract considerable weight to the objective of achieving a reasonable relationship between costs and charges to customers, for this is likely to enhance the attractiveness of the United Kingdom as a place for undertaking international business, and to enhance the competitiveness of business already located here.

Certainly if the experience of British Telecom is any guide, efficiency, never good, has declined, but this may be more due to the fact that there were, initially, few management changes at the upper-levels than to the factor of actual share ownership. More recently, however, there have been major changes, with several thousand managerial posts chopped and a new structure imposed.

By contrast British Gas, which was tightly managed as a nationalized enterprise by the formidable and charismatic Sir Denis Rooke, appears to have increased operating efficiencies against very little competition. In a survey of 1.25 million gas users in 1990, British Gas found that customers awarded it 90 per cent for maintaining gas supplies and attending to leaks, and 71 per cent for dealing with telephone enquiries. This enabled the company to publish a self-congratulatory advertisement, 'Banishing Gripes', stating that 'while most of our customers rate us highly, 2 per cent of you feel we take too long to complete a job'. The advertisement went on to explain how matters were being speeded up to deal with the '2 per cent'.

The survey was the largest of its kind ever conducted by a service industry, and the huge response rate must be seen as encouraging. It certainly enabled Sir Denis' successor as chairman of British Gas, Robert Evans, to promise its customers specific quality targets, possibly backed by financial compensation for inadequate service.

BRITISH PETROLEUM

Whereas little change in management style was apparent in many of the newly-privatized companies, in others there was nothing less than a cultural revolution.

In the spacious management dining-room of British Petroleum's uninspiring head-office building adjoining the Barbican development on the northside of the City of London, executives joked about 'Horticulture' – a reference not to the leafy conservatory across the road, but to the new style introduced into Britain's biggest company by Robert Horton, the chairman.

Horton had shown himself to be a lively character when, as BP's group finance director in the mid-80s, he had pronounced that the giant corporation was 'becoming more of a bank than a trader of oil'. This may have caused some raised eyebrows amongst the traditionalists, but it was true, and Horton, with the help of the able John Browne, had maximized group earnings from financial transactions.

Then Horton and Browne were sent out to Cleveland, Ohio to sort out the mess of Standard Oil which BP was digesting. By the time Horton had created BP America, returned to London, and had taken over the top job, he had some very clear ideas as to what he would do.

The first casualty was the headquarters building itself. Horton decided he did not want such a monolith, but a company operating in smaller units. He wanted to disperse operational staff outside London. BP Exploration was shifted to Glasgow, and young executives in the team found themselves commuting to Scotland during the week while their wives attempted to sell Home Counties homes in a falling property market.

Next to go was the company's command structure. Ever since the Second World War, BP had operated a bureaucratic structure, with dozens of committees and a system whereby the top management undertook their tasks by regularly running the rule over their subordinates. Horton replaced the large, formal and hierarchical departmental structure with smaller, flexible teams, many of them working across several functions and disciplines, and some of them temporary.

At the top level he split the job of his predecessor, Sir Peter Walters, in two, adopting the American 'one-over-one' system and titles. Horton is chairman and chief executive, concentrating mainly on strategy. David Simon, a leading contender for the top job, is deputy chairman and chief operating officer with the daunting task of making sure that the business meets targets.

This system is an innovation in Britain and Europe, though the norm in the United States. However, it is gaining ground, and is starting to appear, in various versions, in a number of companies. It is also a recognition of the fact that large, privatized companies are too big for one person to carry the role of strategic leadership and thinking, and day-to-day number-crunching.

Under Project 1990, Horton is attempting to create a new environment, whereby managers and other employees have more freedom and are placed under a bond of trust. The intention is to replace the reference-upwards procedures of the past with one whereby top management is expected to see its role as challenging decisions rather than making all of them.

Horton admits there is a risk. It is, he says, commonplace for business school academics and management consultants to talk about abandoning hierarchies and replacing them with informal organizations, but 'there are few examples so far of it having been successful on the scale that we are going to do it' (*Financial Times*, 30 March 1990).

Adds Horton's deputy, David Simon: 'We've got to get used to managing by exception, yet picking up the tab. Everyone at the top will find it very difficult – and it's a helluva responsibility for us.'

It is too early to make a judgement as to whether BP will be a better and more profitable company as a result of these changes. At least there have been changes. Non-privatized bodies like British Rail have shown themselves stubbornly resistant to change, and although British Airways improved dramatically while still a state concern, could it not have been the prospect of privatization that motivated it? European airlines that remain in the public sector have shown very little improvement. Perhaps if there is a good management, then it does not matter whether or not a company is in the government or private sector. But a bad management will not be salvaged by privatization.

BRITISH STEEL

Once British Steel was a figure of fun, the nationalized industry that just could not get it right. In the 1979–80 year, British Steel's losses cost the taxpayer £1,700 million. Then the Government brought in a tough American, Sir Ian McGregor, to put in commercial management and run it on modern lines.

By the time it was privatized, it was making a small profit. More to the point, the workforce had been cut by more than 70 per cent, while productivity had risen by 60 per cent.

ARE PRIVATIZED ENTERPRISES MORE COMPETITIVE?

This is an easier question to answer, and it seems to depend on whether they have any serious competition or not.

I believe that the market-place is a more efficient determinant of competition than the various quangoes the Government has established to curb monopoly power. Thus British Airways, which is subject to ruthless competition on the international routes, is not only all the better for it, but also has seen substantial efficiency gains. By contrast, there would be few people who would argue that British Telecom is more efficient.

Of course, it could be argued that the improvements in British Airway's performance are due to a combination of size and market domination (as distinct from monopoly), and the tough and competent management of Sir Colin Marshall. Perhaps if the airline had stayed under Government ownership, it would have achieved the same results?

British Airways argues that it is a highly-competitive airline. It is – when it has to face true competition – such as in one of the toughest markets of all, the North Atlantic, where at least six major American carriers, as well as a number of charter operators, and one or two other international airlines, like Air India, provide rival services from London's three major airports.

But British Airways faces very little competition in Britain, and where it does, it has tried to squash it. Talk with Mike Bishop, the likeable Australian who has built up the new second-force airline, British Midland, and he will tell you that whenever he plans a new route or service, BA tries to block it. Now that privatized BA has absorbed British Caledonian – a deal which was waved through by the Government's magic wand in clear breach of monopoly principles – British Airways is the dominant force at Heathrow, Gatwick, Glasgow and Manchester Airports. It also uses Edinburgh, Prestwick and Aberdeen Airports, and Birmingham. It remains to be seen what its plans are for Stansted, where Air UK is the main domestic carrier.

In Europe, too, BA sometimes presents itself more as a disagreeable monopoly than as a truly competitive airline. By acting in concert with a number of state airlines, such as Alitalia and Air France, its fares are both restrictive and expensive. The doctrine appears to be that when it can get away with operating as a quasi-monopoly, it does so.

Another privatized concern that can hardly be said to be competitive is the British Airports Authority. It has a monopoly on the two largest international airports in the world – London's Heathrow and Gatwick – and when Stansted is expanded in size to become larger than the Surrey airfield, it will have three.

This is another example of the Government creating a private monopoly from a public. Before privatization, in a paper published by the Institute for Fiscal Studies, a number of transport economists argued strongly that Heathrow and Gatwick should be owned by separate companies and forced to compete.

Both airports are overloaded, and there is an urgent need for a new runway, particularly at Gatwick where the single strip for both take-offs and landings raises important safety questions. There are important environmental issues, which can only be resolved by Westminster after the inevitable endless public inquiries. If the BAA ceased to behave as a monopoly, a solution to overcrowding could be found. That solution almost certainly involves the construction of a new airport, probably on the Thames estuary, outside BAA's control. Were such a new airport to be commissioned, BAA would almost certainly overcome its objection to capital investment in new runway capacity.

Its ostrich-like approach, contradicting the Civil Aviation Authority's argument that new capacity is needed because the number of passengers travelling via London's three airports is projected to grow from 60 million in 1989 to between 120 million and 140 million by 2005, is the classic posture of a cosy monopoly. BAA accepts new capacity will be needed, but not yet. Let's push more business through Heathrow, it says. It could have added: That will bring more business to the airline terminals that are little different from out-of-town shopping centres, more business to the car parks monopoly, and more opportunity to raise runway charges that are already above the world average.

All this may be good for shareholders in the short term – and of all the privatized giants, the BAA is the most obsessively short term in its thinking – but its policy is hardly conducive to improving the lot of the travelling public, for which airports are supposed to be designed. In the end it will also damage Britain's economy. At present, the London airports are the most important gateway to Europe: this could be changed if frustrated airline operators switch to Amsterdam, Paris or Brussels. Already, British Airways is planning for that day by joining KLM, the Dutch airline, in taking a strategic stake in the Belgian carrier, Sabena, with the aim of developing Zaventem Airport in Brussels as a major European hub-airport. The French are countering by investing more than £1 billion in improvements to make Charles de Gaulle airport in Paris a major European hub. The BAA will be the ultimate loser.

What happens to BAA wil largely depend on politics. Common sense dictates that it be broken up, and if the Conservatives are re-elected, there is sufficient back-bench support for the idea for the Government to take this step, probably by relinquishing its golden share and allowing market forces to take over. In the meantime, if ever there was a job that should be assigned to the Monopolies and Mergers Commission by the Office of Fair Trading, it is an investigation into the way BAA has used its monopoly to create unjustified profits on duty-free shopping, car parking and fees on hotel buses.

ARE THEY MORE ACCOUNTABLE?

The theory is that privatized concerns are more accountable than a nationalized industry, but so far it is little more than a theory. The shareholders of a nationalized corporation are the Government, and therefore it asks the questions, through civil servants and junior ministers in the appropriate department. There is also the cumbersome apparatus of Parliamentary select committees, whose probes into nationalized industries have given rise to some occasional sharp committee room cross-examination, but few probes of any real depth.

But parliamentarians have made a better job of it than shareholders of the newly-privatized industries, and at least the public had the benefit of press reports and transcripts of select committees. By contrast, most of the information that has passed out of the privatized giants to the media and public has been the sanitized verbosity of glib public relations officers, who see their prime duty as protecting the managements that provide their well-paid employment rather than fulfilling a fiduciary obligation to shareholders. Shareholder relations, in fact, are the preserve of another well-rewarded arm of management, the investor relations officers, who spend most of their time wining and dining fund managers of the big investment institutions.

The opportunity for the ordinary shareholder to challenge the way British Telecom, British Gas, British Steel or British Airways is run are few, and usually limited to the annual meeting. These vary in style, and content. Some, like a Billy Graham revivalist meeting, or a pyramid-selling seminar, are conducted in stadiums or a venue capable of accommodating a large crowd, like the National Exhibition Centre in Birmingham. Others use hotels with conference facilities, and offer shareholders a cup of coffee and a currant bun. British Airways favours the Royal Albert Hall, where the chairman, Lord King of Wartnaby, occupies centre stage and becomes testy if the shareholders ask questions about his own generous remuneration.

British Airways – like many of the others – warms up the crowd with a self-adulatory corporate video, rich in choral sound-effects ideally suited for the hall's splendid accoustics and designed, no doubt, to convince all but the most hard-bitten shareholder that theirs, indeed, is the 'world's favourite airline', and that they should approach the arrival, on the podium, of their directors in a laudable mood. After an 11 o'clock start, Lord King likes to have the meeting finished not long after noon, well in time for a champagne reception and buffet lunch for the media and the representatives of the more important insurance companies, pension funds and other investment institutions. The annual meeting is carried out professionally with great aplomb, but few shareholders are any the wiser than they were when they received their copies of the annual report and accounts.

Few privatized companies spare expense on this annual document for shareholders: I know of one who sent a photographer to the Utah desert to get one shot for the set of magnificent colour illustrations that are now *de rigueur* in such publications. Most cost at least £2.50 a copy to produce and mail out, which can be almost a quarter of the dividend payments to some of the smaller shareholders.

You need a short course in basic accounting to get any real information from any of these documents, but fortunately financial newspapers will cull the more important facts. Very little information of any value will appear in the glossy first half, or in the chairman's review: such useful information as there is will be contained in the accounts and the notes attached to them.

Even if annual shareholders' meetings were an effective means of making a company's directors accountable, the odds are against anything controversial being debated at them. Most boards clear controversial issues out of the way well before the annual meeting, and if a powerful institution feels strongly that directors should be removed because of past failures, resignations and replacements will be engineered and organized well before the formal vote needs to be taken. By that time, the institutions will have mustered sufficient proxy votes to avoid any unpleasantness. That, after all, is the British way of doing things.

Thus, managements are not called upon to account for major blunders. Such was the case with British Telecom, headed by Ian Vallance. One of the BT board's first commercial acts after privatization was to sanction the purchase, in March 1986, for £167 million, of a 51 per cent stake in Mitel, a Canadian company which manufactures private branch exchanges. Four years later, the Canadian stock market valued BT's stake at about one-third of what it had paid for it, and over the period BT had chalked up losses of over £120 million by virtue of its dud investment.

BT's mistake was to assume grandiose ambitions the moment it was privatized. As a nationalized industry, British Telecom had maintained a total grip on the provision of telephone equipment to its subscribers, who were forced to rent telephones at rates which bore no relationship to their cost. British subscribers who visited friends in other countries, particularly the United States and Australia, could only marvel at the range of equipment available there.

This cartel clearly had to be abolished with privatization, and telephone shops opened up in almost every town in the country offering consumers an attractive and competitive range of telephones and accessories. Japanese and American suppliers, in particular, penetrated the market. The same was true of private branch exchanges, or PBXs, where BT's British-made offerings were particularly weak in the market.

So BT decided that it would have to be a totally integrated company, supplying the whole range of telephone equipment and PBXs on a global scale. It clearly could not buy out the British competition – the telecommunications arms of Plessey and Sir Arnold Weinstock's GEC. Mitel, founded in 1971 by two Englishmen, Michael Cowpland and Terry Matthews, seemed the right vehicle for this expansion. It was doing well in the United States, but needed more funds for research and development, and commercial exploitation; it was an entrepreneurial company; and its products would allow BT to be both network provider and manufacturer, and hence dominate the market in Britain.

So used were the senior management of British Telecom to running a monopoly that it did not occur to them that some people might take exception to a strategy which allowed the company to flex its muscles so quickly. Or, if they did, they thought that they would get away with it.

GEC's Sir Arnold Weinstock had other ideas, and protests to the Government quickly led to the referral of the proposed acquisition of Mitel to the Monopolies and Mergers Commission on the grounds that it might be against the public interest.

The MMC has never been an easy organization to deal with, and it does not like to come to conclusions in a hurry. Some of its members have a penchant for pedantry. When it did come to a conclusion, it accepted that the takeover of Mitel could well be against the public interest, but its members were divided on detailed recommendations, and two reports were produced. The majority favoured allowing BT to proceed; the minority recommended the move be blocked.

The majority recommendation stripped from BT one of the main advantages of buying Mitel: for it sought to impose a condition that BT should have to wait four years before supplying Mitel equipment to British customers. Although this condition was watered down by Leon Brittan, the then Trade and Industry Secretary, BT found its hands severely tied.

Any other commercial enterprise would have pulled out at

this stage, but the MMC report had taken so long to produce that the normal 90-day due diligence time had elapsed and BT behaved as might be expected of a large bureaucratic organization, and honoured its commitment. 'We were trapped,' a BT executive recalled. 'By this time Mitel's finances had deteriorated, and the *raison d'être* for the takeover had vanished, but we felt we were too heavily committed to back out.'

In the end, the very things that had attracted BT to Mitel mitigated against it. BT, again behaving like a large oligarchy, decided that Cowpland and Matthews had committed far too much money to R and D and cut the budgets back. Projects were folded, and staff morale collapsed with them. Key people left the company, convinced that there was no future for them in an organization like British Telecom. Their decision seems justified, for there was no attempt to cross-pollinate managers between the two organizations. Mitel's figures got worse, and the minority shareholders began to trade in their holdings.

By January 1990, British Telecom had decided it wanted to wash its hands of Mitel, and was preparing to write off the loss in its books. David Dey, the managing director of BT's communications division, announced a new strategy: BT would stick to services. 'Criticism that we had no experience in mergers and acquisitions, or of manufacturing, are, with hindsight, justified,' he told the magazine *Management Today*. 'We now have a new strategy, concentrating on our core business – networking – and of turning to major suppliers for products.

'We have been looking for a world supplier who would give us exclusive distribution in the UK and the same rights worldwide. We believe we have found this with Northern Telecom.'

Thus, another near-monopoly was in the creation. It still did not occur to BT that it might be better to deal with a whole range of suppliers. Or that such a deal would be regarded as anti-competitive in the United States. Not that it matters. As a major competitor of BT told *Management Today*, 'Competition policy in the UK means that there is really very little competition. BT still has not been tempered by the true competitive environment.'

Meanwhile, BT has lost its shareholders many millions of pounds. Ian Vallance, at the time of writing, is still in at the helm.

· 18 ·

Curbing the monopolies

'I'm here because I'm needed by customers to ensure there is no exploitation'
– Ian Byatt, director-general of the Office of Water

'I can't shoot from the hip all the time'
– Bryan Carlsberg, director-general of the Office of Telecommunications

'It would be a mistake to think we will be confronting the British Gas Corporation. Our job is to ensure it carries out what it is supposed to do'
– James McKinnon, director-general of the Office of Gas Supply

MANY IMAGINED THAT by privatizing the nationalized industries the Government was abdicating control of them, and abandoning them to market forces. This was far from the case. Each privatization was accompanied by the introduction of a new regulatory apparatus. And, in many instances, the Government retained total control with its ownership of a golden share.

A golden share works like a preference share, although it is much more powerful and even more undemocratic. The way a government-owned golden share works is to place stringent restrictions on the other shareholders, especially in their right to sell their holdings. (The restrictions are published in the *Pathfinder* prospectus.)

More significantly, golden shares have been used to enforce codes and rules imposed on the new privatized companies by their own articles of association. Normally a company's articles of association may be changed by the calling of an extraordinary general meeting of shareholders and a 75 per cent vote. But by giving the golden share a right of veto on any change in articles of association, the Government can effectively veto any eventuality written into the articles. The holder of a golden share is normally the appropriate secretary of state, who therefore holds absolute power.

The Government retains a golden share indefinitely in British Telecom, British Gas, British Aerospace, Cable & Wireless, aero-engine manufacturer Rolls-Royce (not to be confused with Rolls-Royce motors, which is part of the Vickers group), BAA, National Power, PowerGen, the National Grid, Sealink and shipbuilders VSEL.

There are a variety of reasons why it does so. Some are associated with the nation's security: Whitehall does not want high-technology companies like British Aerospace, Rolls-Royce or Cable & Wireless to pass into foreign hands; and it also would be worrying if telecommunications or gas supplies were not under domestic control. At the time of the Falklands War, the Government commandeered some of the cross-Channel ferries to tranship troops and equipment to the South Atlantic: if it had not had a golden share in Sealink, it would have had to pass legislation to do so.

The Government's special share in Sealink prevents the shareholders from disposing of it, or from selling more than 25 per cent of its fleet. The company cannot be wound up without the approval of the Secretary of State for Transport.

In most cases, the permanent golden share limits individual or overseas ownership to 15 per cent of the total stock. But not all golden shares are permanent: sometimes the Government has given them a limited life of five or ten years. In these instances, the issue of a golden share has not been to protect the national interest, or to ensure security, but to assist the organization during a difficult transition to the private sector, so that it does not fall prey to predators, particularly from North America or Japan.

The Government retains a golden share in the ten privatized water companies, mainly to stop them being taken over by the French, who have made ownership of water a speciality. For the first five years of their life, no one shareholder may hold more than 15 per cent of any water company. The Government will retain the golden share for the second five years, but will then permit higher levels of ownership, provided that 75 per cent of the shareholders approve. Mindful of Welsh nationalism and the heavy rain on the Welsh mountains, the Government will keep a golden share in Welsh Water permanently.

Companies in which the Government decided not to have a golden share include British Airways and Associated British Ports.

After some controversy, it gave up its golden share in Jaguar, the car maker, and in Britoil, when it was taken over by British Petroleum. The removal of the stake in Jaguar allowed the two American car makers, General Motors and Ford, to conduct a battle for control of the company, which Ford eventually won. The institutions and the arbitrageurs made the money on the deal, not the small shareholders in the Midlands.

At the time of writing, there was an issue of whether or not the golden share in BAA would be retained by Whitehall. Since there is no golden share on Britain's ports, it seems illogical to maintain one over the monopoly controlling the major airports. If the share is released, the BAA almost certainly will be turned over on the stock markets and broken up.

THE REGULATORS

Because privatization has turned public monopolies into private ones, the Government has created a new breed of referee whose job it is to try and ensure fair play. Heading organizations with strange-sounding acronyms, like OFWAT, OFGAS or OFFER, these men have tended to behave more like regulators than watchdogs. They do not give the impression of being *proactive* – poking their noses into the businesses of the privatized giants. Rather, they seem to be *reactive* – waiting for either members of the public or competitors to complain, and then investigating the complaints, within the strict parameters of the appropriate legislation.

Perhaps that is what was intended: after all, Britain has Sir Gordon Borrie's Office of Fair Trading to act as ferret, although its budget and staff are clearly insufficient for it to be as effective as its chief would wish it to be. But, given that the British Government has put into place some of Europe's largest private companies – and endowed them with many special privileges and protection, as well as sweeping monopoly powers – it is surprising that these referees have been provided with such weak whistles that they are barely heard.

The regulators also have only limited powers. They can issue warnings, but they cannot shut a business down. Real power remains with government ministers. This is rather like allowing a soccer referee to show a yellow warning card, but not to send to the dressing-room a player who ignores the warning without consulting the manager first.

Not surprisingly, the jobs available have attracted administrators rather than entrepreneurs, desk-men rather than detectives. Only Bryan Carlsberg, at the Office of Telecommunications, seems to want to speak out, or become embroiled in controversy: the others seem more didactic, more in the mould of a civil servant straight out of *Yes Minister*. Some of them were involved in fashioning the organizations they are now regulating. This is all right when the new corporation breaks the rules, but what happens when it behaves badly within the law because the law-makers did not anticipate certain conduct? No judge likes to gainsay a piece of case history which he or she put into the law books.

The most important task shared by all the regulators is the supervision of price-increases. This clearly cannot be left to the privatized quasi-monopoly. In most cases, price-increases are tied to the rise in the Retail Price Index, with a variant up or down depending on special external factors or the need to ensure that the organization increases productivity. The regulators will be subject to intensive lobbying by the organization – and by others, including politicians anxious to keep prices down so as to win elections.

Another task is obtaining information from the concern. When he was chairman of British Gas, the tetchy Sir Denis Rooke made little secret of his reluctance to pass on facts and figures to OFGAS: indeed, the acrimony between regulator and chairman in earlier privatizations was such that the Government wrote information requirements into the Water Bill and Electricity Bill.

While there are similarities, there are also widespread differences between the major regulators. At OFFER, the Birmingham-based Office of Electricity Regulation, Professor Stephen Littlechild, an economist, watches over 19 separate electricity companies, including the state-owned Nuclear Electric and Scottish Nuclear. 'My job is to adjudicate between the parties rather than to take up the burden of overseeing one major licensee,' he says.

OFFER has also to make sure that there is no collusion between the various electricity companies through cross-subsidies or price-fixing. This may not be easy. On the generating side in England and Wales, the two major companies, National Power and PowerGen, were born out of the ashes of the old Central Electricity Generating Board, and most of those working for them were former colleagues at the CEGB.

OFFER has some teeth for the maltreated consumer. For example, if the standard of service provided by the regional distributing companies – formerly the area boards – falls below certain specified standards, OFFER can order them to pay compensation to the customer. These payments are likely to come into play when, for example, a customer is disconnected from the system for no apparent reason.

The prize for the most combatative and most visible of the regulators would have to be shared between James McKinnon, director-general of the Office of Gas Supply and Bryan Carlsberg, director-general of the Office of Telecommunications

OFTEL works from an undistinguished building in London's Holborn district, and Carlsberg's office is an acute contrast with the modern luxury of Ian Vallance's suite in British Telecom's expensive headquarters in the City. Carlsberg, in his early 50s, is ideally qualified for the tough job he has taken on until at least 1992. Besides being a professional accountant, he is a marathon runner, and prior to coming to the job, he had bad experiences with the telephone service. So he feels for people who have endured bad service, understands BT's delphic accounting practices, and has the endurance for a long battle.

Carlsberg graduated at the London School of Economics just down the road from his present office, did his articles at Deloittes, and then established his own accountancy practice in Hertfordshire, where he was told by the Post Office that it would take a year to get a phone line. He wrote to the Post Office Minister at the time, and the line was in within three weeks: 'I learned how to complain early on.'

Carlsberg found accountancy too restrictive, and went back to the LSE as a lecturer in accounting. For a while he was in the United States as a visiting lecturer, and while there joined the US Financial Accounting Standards Board as assistant lecturer. When he returned to the LSE, his services were in demand as a consultant, and he advised the responsible minister, Kenneth Baker, on privatization. Within months, he was seen as the right person to run OFTEL, which now has 120 people on staff to deal with the complaints, technical problems and complex regulatory issues that flow into the office.

Under his leadership, OFTEL has some achievements to its credit. One was the impending introduction of itemized accounts for those who requested it: a benefit BT once said was impossible, until Mercury beat them to it.

SELLING THE FAMILY SILVER

OFGAS – AND THE GASBUSTER

The British gas consumer has good cause to thank James McKinnon, the Scots accountant who has headed the Office of Gas Supply since its establishment. But for him gas prices would be higher, and British Gas would still be sheltering behind the protective monopolistic shell with which the Government foolishly endowed it upon privatization. McKinnon refused to be cowed by the dominant Sir Denis Rooke in a bruising public confrontation between the two men, and eventually won his battle to force British Gas to become more open.

On the other hand, whether Sid, the celebrated private shareholder, has such cause to celebrate McKinnon's battles on behalf of the consumer is very debatable. But for McKinnon, British Gas would undoubtedly be making bigger profits – or harbouring more fat cats in its management – and Sid might be getting bigger dividends.

In privatizing British Gas, the Government wanted to offer both Sid and the institutions a real carrot – the prospect of monopoly profits for years to come – and did so. It also did not want to upset Sir Denis, the fiery chief of British Gas, whose ability to suffer fools – and civil servants – was widely known to be extremely limited. Rooke made it clear he did not want too much truck with bureaucrats from the Department of Energy, and he had even less time for those who made their living in and around the Stock Exchange.

So, in framing the Gas Act, both the Government and its advisers did everything possible to placate Sir Denis. British Gas would be the only authorized gas supplier. British Gas was not obliged to disclose the size of the composition of its monopoly profits from domestic consumers. It was under no obligation to buy in cheap surplus gas from competitors at times of low demand, an essential condition for increased competition. It was permitted to cross-subsidize industrial customers from its other operations. The price of domestic gas was to be fixed by a simple formula: it could go up by the rise in the consumer price index, minus x per cent (where x was a percentage designed to force British Gas to squeeze its costs), plus y (where y was any increase in the price of North Sea gas). Non-domestic gas prices were subjected only to general scrutiny or no regulation at all.

When McKinnon, with his unmistakable Glaswegian accent, moved into modest offices in London's Victoria Street, he knew that OFGAS and its staff of about 30 had relatively few powers. Life would be very different from his previous post as finance director of the Imperial Group. But he had some kind of affinity with Rooke: after all, both disliked the short-termism of the City, which had dictated the passing of Imperial into the hands of Lord Hanson, a move he had opposed. He hoped he would not have to use the one set of teeth the Government had provided OFGAS with: the right to go to the Monopolies and Mergers Commission if British Gas denied him information on domestic pricing.

But it was not long before the sparks began to fly. After only just over six months since moving into the job, McKinnon suspected that the 4.5 per cent cut in domestic prices announced by British Gas was not enough. Oil and gas prices had fallen fast: gas in Britain was significantly more expensive than in other countries. Despite several polite formal and informal requests, British Gas refused to provide information on how the new prices had been fixed. Senior management had been rewarded with pay-increases averaging 46 per cent – with Rooke being paid £184,000, 68 per cent more than pre-privatization – yet gas workers' salaries had moved only in line with inflation, and productivity had increased. So what was going on?

The letters to British Gas from OFGAS became more and more terse, and the replies briefer. It was only a matter of time before the dispute became public. 'If you have issues between you and you cannot solve them privately, then you have to solve them publicly,' McKinnon said later. On 28 July 1987, OFGAS officially told journalists that it was considering legal action because British Gas had refused to supply its forecast for the average price it paid for its gas, the key component in calculating the gas tariff. 'A series of angry letters has been exchanged' and an impasse reached, said OFGAS. British Gas retorted that it was 'not going to give any more details; we have already given them more than we have to'.

McKinnon offered to visit British Gas headquarters to look at the data he needed under conditions of confidentiality, but his request was refused. An editorial in the *Financial Times* commented: 'The company responded with the arrogance which might be expected of an entrenched monopoly.'

The head of OFGAS returned from a tour of Britain's regions and reported that British Gas was widely seen as bureaucratic and uncaring. And more than 100 industrial users surveyed by OFGAS reported that they would like to find an alternative supplier. McKinnon said he would ask the Monopolies and Mergers Commission to intervene.

The scene was set for a show-down. On 27 August, the annual meeting of British Gas was due to take place at the National Exhibition Centre in Birmingham. More than 6,000 shareholders were expected to turn up. Hordes of British Gas staff were moved into Birmingham to deal with both public and Press. A translator was engaged to provide speeches in sign language for the deaf. There were exhibitions and side-shows, including the British Gas intelligent pig – not an automated meter-reader, but a device for cleaning pipelines. Because of the large crowd expected, an overspill facility had been arranged in an adjoining hall. The media turned up in large numbers, anticipating a show in which Sir Denis might be at his most entertaining. The previous day, he had reportedly told an analyst who had asked a question about the OFGAS request to 'get knotted'.

But the show-down never took place. With a fine sense of timing, on the morning of the meeting, British Gas hand-delivered to OFGAS an envelope containing the figures sought. In Birmingham, only half the expected crowd turned up, and not one person asked a question about the matter. Sir Denis kept his cool, and the shareholders took their free coffee and biscuits and departed happily.

The truce turned out only to be temporary, for McKinnon then inevitably turned his attention to industrial gas prices, assisted by a complaint from Sheffield Forgemasters, which complained that British Gas was overcharging its customers. At a conference on the privatized gas industry, organized by Public Issue Conferences, the OFGAS director accused British Gas of excessive secrecy, and suggested it should publish its prices as a stable tariff. British Gas, said McKinnon, was 'not a barrow boy, but a very large company'.

When the Monopolies and Mergers Commission's report was published in the Autumn of 1988, the Sheffield Forgemasters complaint was upheld. British Gas, reported the MMC, was boosting profits 'through extensive discrimination' in its sales in favour of customers whose consumption was big enough to enable them to buy gas elsewhere.

High gas prices in Britain, stated the MMC, were a cause of real concern: 'If there were competition for the supply of gas, it is unlikely that this degree of price discrimination could be maintained.'

The Government took its time to study the report, but in the end accepted most of its findings. It also bowed to pressure and gave OFGAS long overdue control over industrial, as well as domestic, pricing. Discriminatory pricing came to an end.

For those interested in pursuing the history of this subject further, the MMC report pulls no punches and makes fascinating reading, confirming the mistakes made by the Government in the way it privatized gas by allowing British Gas such a monopoly. The sadness is that the report was conducted after privatization, and not before it. And, but for McKinnon, the inquiry would not have taken place at all.

The *Financial Times* commented: 'The old nationalized industries' arrogance and their insensitivity to wider economic costs will take time and the determined effort of regulators to break down, as is now evident in British Telecom as well as British Gas.'

As a postcript to this salutary tale, I am pleased to report that McKinnon has battled on. In the Spring of 1989, Sir Denis, by then 65, took retirement. By making British Gas one of the few truly successful nationalized industries, he had much to his credit. But he never really liked privatization, or the new light it shed on the darker corners of British Gas.

Rooke was replaced by his deputy, the less cantankerous Robert Evans, who promised to be more democratic and more diplomatic. In early 1990, Evans appointed ombudsmen in each of the 12 regions with the power to award compensation of up to £5,000 a time to any of British Gas' 17 million customers receiving poor service. He seems to have established a much better relationship with McKinnon than did his predecessor, though the OFGAS director has shown no signs of letting-up.

In his 1990 report, McKinnon said serious complaints about British Gas had almost doubled. One major gripe was that in some areas British Gas had estimated bills for two to three years without making a meter reading. British Gas was retorting with its familiar complacency. 'We have learned to live with the sort of comments OFGAS makes,' said a British Gas statement.

I doubt it, and I am glad.

· 19 ·

Doing it elsewhere

PRIVATIZATION IS IN fashion the world over. From Madrid to Mexico City, from Toronto to Togo, from Innsbruck to Islamabad, national and local governments are selling off businesses once thought of as essential to the national interest to be owned by the state.

Privatization has become a billion dollar industry – and British merchant banks, accountancy firms and law firms stand to make the biggest killing. Some, like the London-based accountancy firm Price Waterhouse, have formed separate departments of privatization services, designed to offer consultancy and specialist advice worldwide to governments contemplating following in Margaret Thatcher's footsteps.

Howard Hyman, the firm's director of privatization services, believes that any activity providing goods or services of measurable worth is now a candidate – including education and health. 'The question being asked now is not "Why do we need to privatize this?" but "Why does the government need to own it?"'

Privatization is by no means confined to anti-socialist governments, although the rapid sell-off of state enterprises in France was abruptly halted when Jacques Chirac's government fell to the Socialists. However, the left-of-centre Michel Rocard did not reverse the trend, and renationalize. And some countries with social democratic governments, like Denmark, the Netherlands, Israel, Italy, Malaysia and New Zealand, all have major plans to dispose of state businesses.

Elsewhere, Turkey is planning to denationalize its 263 state companies. Nigeria wants to privatize its 160 state-owned banks, all the breweries and the insurance industry. Argentina is selling off its telecommunications utility, ENtel. Mexico has shed over 300 state institutions, and plans to rid itself of the national airline, Mexicana.

Perhaps the most unexpected convert to privatization is Pakistan. Pakistan's first elected Prime Minister, Ali Bhutto, took over all the country's banks and major industries in one night in 1972. Mr Bhutto's daughter, Benazir, who won government from the man who put her father to death, General Zia al Huk, introduced a policy of privatizing these same state enterprises. The reason: in her years of exile in Britain Ms Bhutto studied Mrs Thatcher's privatization policies, and vowed to introduce them into her own country.

Almost her first act upon attaining office was to commission Rothschilds, the London merchant bank that had handled so successfully the British Gas sale, to undertake a study of an extensive privatization programme. This was by no means an easy task given that in 1988 public sector corporations sustained an aggregate loss of £350 million – an insignificant figure by British standards, but huge for Pakistan.

The problem Rothschilds immediately faced was not so much identifying which companies should be sold off, but assessing whether there was sufficient liquid capital in Pakistan to fund the sales. Pakistan, not the most stable of Asian democracies, has one of the lowest savings ratios in the world; private investment, where it exists, is heavily in property; and many Pakistanis have sought to smuggle their assets overseas.

A major problem is that the state corporations, many of them inefficient, corrupt and overstaffed, do not have a good image. When Bhutto attempted to raise just £30 million by selling bearer bonds in the Water and Power Development Authority (WAPDA), the largest public sector corporation in Pakistan, the issue flopped, leaving the banks to buy them. 'WAPDA does not have a good image. Nobody has confidence in it, so why should they buy its bonds', was the forthright explanation of

Meekhal Asia Ahmad, chief economist of the country's planning commission. 'It is vital the first sale should be successful, that we begin with something with a good reputation and track record that will sell like hot cakes.' (*Financial Times*, 19 July 1989.)

Rothschilds recommended that privatization should be handled in the same manner as in Britain – by undertaking sell-offs step-by-step – so as not to place too great a strain on a thin market. Ms Bhutto, under pressure from an agreement with the International Monetary Fund to bring the budget deficit down to 5.5 per cent of gross domestic product, would have liked to have raised up to £100 million in the first year, 1990, but accepted the banker's approach, and has published a short list of companies to be sold. They include the Sul Gas Transmission Corporations, Pakistan State Oil, the Habib Bank and Pakistan International Airlines, all deemed to have a reasonable prospect of financial success. The IMF set the reduction of the budget deficit as a priority condition for advancing.

Twelve of the 14 sectors in which Pakistan's 69 public sector corporations operate are thought to be profitable, but some state bodies are deemed as almost beyond redemption. The National Construction Corporation, a body that was responsible for well over one-third of the total public sector losses, was liquidated, the first time a loss-making organization in the state sector had been folded. There are severe question marks over the National Shipping Corporation and the National Development Corporation.

In Pakistan, privatization is in the hands of a National Disinvestment Authority, advised by Rothschilds, but with a brief to try and follow the Swedish example of strong employee participation.

In Sweden, about 87 per cent of industry is privately owned, but there are the employee funds, which the Swedish government introduced to give workers a stake in industry. After certain deductions for reinvestment, 20 per cent of net profits are allocated to these funds.

But Ajaz Ahmed, vice chairman of the National Disinvestment Authority, fears that Pakistani workers are more interested in higher wages than share allocations. He also believes that, as in Britain, strong incentives need to be given to attract investors. 'Why should they invest when they can put money in savings schemes which guarantee 15 per cent interest?' he asks rhetorically, adding his belief that the government should guarantee a 20 per cent dividend for the first five years until 'people are share minded'. (*Financial Times*, 19 July 1989.)

Across the border in India, a totally different approach is being taken. Privatization is starting at local, rather than national, level and the emphasis is not so much on dismantling the whole apparatus of state, but on using private funds to build badly needed infrastructure.

The pioneer state of Maharashtra, whose principal city is Bombay, is in danger of throttling itself because of lack of essential funds to finance road building, port expansion and power generation. Industrial growth in the state is the highest in India, at between 8 and 9 per cent, but the politicians would like to see it higher, at around 12 per cent, to try and increase income and reduce poverty. But the roads and ports are choked, and there is not enough electricity.

The chemicals and engineering group RPG Enterprises, headed by Harsh Goenka, plans to build a new £72-million four-lane highway from Bombay out through the city's congested industrial belt to Nashik which would be paid for mostly by tolls. It has also a scheme to build a 500-megawatt power plant at Nagpur. Another conglomerate, Reliance Industries, has its eye on Maharashtra's other main road – the highway between Bombay and Pune – as well as two power projects.

Unlike Pakistan, the savings ratio in India is relatively high; the Bombay stock exchange is buoyant, with a record number of new issues tapping the market in 1989. It is not unusual for bank deposits to rise by 20 per cent each year. And Indians can see the virtue of supporting new ventures such as those mentioned, because it will increase output and jobs.

However, India has a problem which Pakistan does not face: its central government in Delhi is much less flexible and slower to move than Ms Bhutto's administration. Delhi is also seriously concerned that the country's power equipment industry will not be able to turn out the generators needed, and that these will have to be imported, expensively, from Europe or Japan. But at the end of 1989, a deal had been worked out whereby private companies would put up power plants (David Housego, *Financial Times*, 27 June 1989). This included a 15 per cent post-tax return on capital based on power plants working at about 63 per cent of capacity. Though the operators will have to accept government-imposed tariffs – as indeed is still the case in Britain because of the K-factor – private businesses hope to make more profit by increasing their load factors.

Another convert to privatization is Malaysia's nationalist and unorthodox Prime Minister, Dr Mahathir Mohamad. A few years ago, Dr Mahathir was bent on moving his country as far away as possible from any concept or idea that had been developed in Britain. He felt the former British colony was still too dependent on the commerce of its former masters, and introduced a policy called 'Look East'. This was designed to encourage Malaysians to put aside any bad British habits they had adopted and opt for the Japanese work ethic.

Since some older Malaysians still remembered the harrowing days of Japanese occupation – while others had the more recent memory of confrontation with communist guerrillas supported by Sukarno's Indonesia – this policy was not an instant success. 'Malaysia Inc', another catch-phrase for another policy of partnership between the state and private enterprise, was not a winner either. State production proved exceptionally inefficient, and businesses run by the minority Chinese tended to do much better than those run by the majority Malays.

Privatization Mahathir-style has a curiously Thatcherite ring about it, even though it seeks to achieve it without too much resort to Western ideology. Mahathir is most anxious to achieve a real people's capitalism, spreading share ownership as widely as possible rather than to large special interest groups. This will produce some interesting conflicts, for government enterprises have traditionally been a major source of employment for young Malays. As efficiencies grow, young Malays will find fewer openings in the public sector, and will have to turn more towards commercial enterprises for employment.

Privatization does seem to have introduced efficiencies, in

companies like the Malaysian Airlines System, and in shipping companies and cement manufacturers. And Malaysian Telecom now manages to install phone lines in two weeks rather than two months: a lesson for British Telecom.

Even in Africa and Latin America, whose economies provide the darkest blot on the world scene, privatization is taking a slow hold. Partly this is because there is very little choice. Having written off billions of dollars of debt in loans to Third World countries, the world's commercial banks are not inclined to extend further credit to regimes run either by unpleasant military juntas or Marxist-Leninist dictators.

The World Bank, under a succession of American presidents, has ceased to be a soft touch, and is actively trying to encourage the establishment of equity markets, and the reintroduction of 'international investment with a human face'.

The World Bank officially favours privatization as a means of reviving the ailing economies of Third World countries, although it is not specific as to the means by which this should be achieved. However, in recent years, its president, Barber Conable, has advocated a move away from aid and debt finance to equity-based schemes to fund new projects in the developing countries.

Yet the World Bank does not believe outright privatization totally dominated by market forces would be the answer – because the result would be a return to colonialism and exploitation.

Its 1990 World Development Report argued for efficient growth based on labour-intensive industries and market incentives. The first of these goals is relatively easy to achieve because only small sums of capital investment are needed to increase output. In many cases, the low labour rates in many countries mean that it would be possible to introduce technology that has been superseded in much of Europe and Japan, but which would still allow for substantial productivity gains. An example of this would be some personal computers, which are now being replaced by faster and smaller machines in the industrialized world, but which still offer major savings in administration.

The second goal – market incentives – is the hardest to create, because these are dependent on increased free trade and on a successful conclusion to the present Uruguay round of negotiations under the auspices of the General Agreement on Tariffs and Trade, due to conclude in December 1990. Unless Third World countries can be given free access to markets in Europe, North America and Japan, their products will not be sold, and privatization will not work.

So it may not be long before multinational companies with a good record in Africa – like Unilever, ICI and Peugeot – are invited back to revitalize stagnant industries.

Tanzania, once a model for African Socialism, is seeking foreign managers for its tourist industry, while the Marxist-Leninists that control Angola, Benin and Congo are trying to sell off state loss-makers. Even Fidel Castro's Cuba is selling houses to tenants.

Mozambique, another haven for Marxists, has already privatized more than 20 industrial companies. But no one has done more than tiny Togo, as confirmed by Koffi Djondo, the Minister for Industry: 'We now have a liberal economy: we are not going to put another franc into state companies.'

For many countries, privatization is not so much a matter of choice but of necessity. In Argentina, for example, where inflation *each week* edges up to the OECD *annual* average, the nationalized industries are costing the country dear.

In 1989, there was a deficit of US$3,867 billion in the nationalized sector, with the telecommunications company ENtel accounting for one-third of this. Who would want to buy it? President Carlos Menem apparently believes there is someone, somewhere, who would like to take on the thankless task of modernizing his country's phone system, for he has commissioned Ms Maria Julia Alsogaray (a government minister) with selling off 60 per cent of ENtel. Perhaps he has in mind to find someone like the hapless Alan Bond, the Australian entrepreneur who persuaded himself that the Chilean telephone system needed his special brand of ownership.

President Menem brands his privatization programme as ambitious, which it undoubtedly is, but for reasons other than those with the official imprimatur. Already one six-month deadline for floating ENtel has passed, as will others. Those with the heart and the nerve to risk their funds on the new candidate for the Buenos Aires stock market are offered a 'guaranteed' 16 per cent return on a net asset value of US$1,900 million, a figure that is but an estimate. Just how accurate an estimate it is must be judged against the fact that a few months earlier, its value had been put at US$3,500 million. Such are the vagaries of hyper-inflation.

The democratically-elected Argentinian government has not, however, been without guile. Those overseas governments and banks who have lent money to Argentina, and who, presumably, see very little chance of ever getting it back, have been invited to retire the debt in favour of equity in ENtel. At the time of writing, syndicates of banks and telecommunications companies from the United States and several European countries were vying for the prize of 60 per cent of ENtel. The only problem is that the winner was being expected to invest another US$4,000 million over the next decade.

If this works – or even if it does not – Menem was planning to move on to float the national airline, Aerolineas Argentinas, on the same system. The government thinks the airline is worth over US$250 million, and wants to sell all but a minor part of it. Perhaps Lord King will buy it.

· 20 ·

A farewell to Karl Marx

'Bureaucracy is one of the main inhibitors of innovation. Just the sheer amount of paperwork required to do anything discourages action. New organizational forms and more experimentation are needed. There has to be a way of creating smaller units within large organizations, of making it easier for small entities to be created'
– Agnes Cseresnyes, Hungarian National Development Bank

'Romania is the furthest behind. It has been hard to own a private cow there, let alone a private company'
– *The Economist* newspaper

'Expectations were too high, and then they fell too fast'
– Zbigniew Lis, acting chairman of Solidarity, the Polish trades union

WELL BEFORE MIKHAIL Gorbachev's wind of change through the Soviet Union and Eastern Europe, one of Russia's satellites, Hungary, was already developing a taste for private enterprise. Peasants working on collective farms were allowed their own allotments. Although the land area covered by these allotments was but a tiny proportion of the hectares under cultivation, the output created by individuals toiling long after normal working hours and selling their products in local markets was substantially greater.

Hungary developed an international agency based in tax-efficient Luxemburg to help it with access to Western technology and markets, and to allow it to invest overseas. It opened the first stock market in the communist world, and allowed Western mutual funds to invest in the country's enterprises. And Hungary developed entrepreneurs.

One of these is Agnes Cseresnyes, managing director of the Unicbank. She was previously the pioneering spirit of the Hungarian National Development Bank, responsible for a number of investment projects in the country that brought together government bodies, building contractors and other shareholders in new ventures.

One new venture was Medinvest. It would have been a lesson for Britain's Conservative government even today. Formed as a new entity under Cseresnyes' leadership after some effective lobbying, Medinvest managed to rebuild and renovate the giant Laszlo Hospital in Budapest in two years, when previously it would have taken a decade.

Medinvest was a consortium of the National Development Bank, Medicor (the main producers of medical equipment), a planning company and two large building contractors. Each had a shareholding in the enterprise whose objective was to make hospital construction or repair more efficient. Instead of a large vertical bureaucracy like Britain's National Health Service, hamstrung by government cutbacks and civil service routines, Medinvest simply got on with the job in hand. Its success was such that Cseresnyes was able to initiate similar consortia to work in school building and transport infrastructure.

Now, with the possible exception of East Germany, a special case because of the help afforded it by the West Germans, Hungary is the pioneer of privatization in Eastern Europe. Like Poland, it is committed to shedding state assets, convinced that only private enterprise, prepared to take real financial risks, will be able to run government businesses.

Speed is essential, for unless there is a rapid change in the economic culture of Eastern Europe, which can only be brought about through privatization, the reforms will not work. Once enterprises in the former Soviet bloc are exposed to market forces and external competition, many of them will collapse since they only exist as a result of state subsidies. Yet speed has generated big problems, particularly in Hungary, where 'spontaneous privatization' is the catch-phrase.

Until 1988, two-thirds of the country's state corporations were run by enterprise councils, whose members comprised of workers' representatives and their managements. These councils were given the right to turn their concerns into joint-stock companies, provided they obtained an audit for the assets and found investors prepared to buy one-fifth of the equity. They then automatically became directors, and were able to pocket some of the cash, handing the rest over to the government. It was a licence to print money – though no more so than some of the fees handed over to City of London advisers in Britain – and in the first year alone, 1,600 new companies were formed by this method.

But, as *The Economist* newspaper reported in April 1990:

The new laws were subjected to creative interpretation, particularly the parts about auditing. How does one put market values on land, buildings, or expertise in a country with no markets? One Polish method is to take the value of a building in 1945, and multiply it by a more or less arbitrary figure for inflation since then. Western auditors like Price Waterhouse and Arthur Anderson have been hard at work in Hungary, but even their attempts at objectivity cannot replace the care a real owner would take to get a fair price. In Hungary, with the enterprise council determining the sale price of assets that it had got for free, tricks of under-valuation opened a large window for corruption.

The same edition of *The Economist* reported how the council of HungarHotels, a chain that owned the Budapest Hyatt and most of the country's best hotels and restaurants, tried to sell half of its equity to a Swedish firm for US$110 million, when one hotel alone was reckoned to be worth US$60 million. In this case the deal was blocked by the Hungarian supreme court.

In other instances, peculiar patterns of cross-ownership, often leaving the parent company as a debt-ridden shell, were used by the former managers to disguise the fact that they were maintaining control of their old companies without either investing new capital or forcing their subsidiaries to compete with one another. *The Economist* reported:

Such confusion about who owned the companies led many investors, especially from the West, to insist on buying them from someone other than the enterprise council. Complex arrangements were set up to meet this demand, with phoney holding companies, and sales and re-sales of shares. Huge sums could be made by those who understood the complicated laws. The offices of the Finance Ministry emptied as their occupants, discovering this, took off for the greener fields of post-Communist merger and acquisition practice.

Western companies are learning to play the game, as when the Austrian bank, Girozentrale, bought 50 per cent of the Tungsram light-bulb company for $110 million, the remainder being bought by an Hungarian bank. Girozentrale then resold its shares to General Electric for $150 million. Eyebrows were raised in Hungary, where some thought the original price too low. But at least money did land in the state treasury, and part of Girozentrale's $40 million profit will go back into Tungsram, so there may be little cause for complaint.

The provisional Hungarian government decided in the Spring of 1990 that this process of spontaneous privatization had gone too far, and established a privatization agency under parliamentary control to try and ensure fair play. All asset sales must now be conducted in public, or with the agency's approval.

The Polish government has also established a similar privatization agency, which selects companies to be sold off from the

7,000 state corporations, and then conducts each sale in public. Unlike the Thatcherite government, small investors are given absolute priority, and the big institutions and overseas buyers may have to wait until a secondary market is established to buy their slice of the action. Employees are given especially favoured treatment. For example, the members of Solidarity working at the former Lenin shipyard in Gdansk were able to buy one-fifth of the total equity at half-price.

The Poles are being more cautious than the Hungarians about the speed of privatization, and the agency has, with one notable exception, followed the Thatcher rule and picked winners for floating-off. But the new government has also introduced one sensible innovation which could well be applied in Britain, and that is to allow workers in state companies that are not yet ripe for privatization to buy small stakes in the business. Couldn't this be applied to British Rail?

Poland has also been the scene of one of privatization's greatest disappointments. The Lenin shipyard at Gdansk was the cradle of the upheavals in Eastern Europe that led to the eventual evaporation of the Communist dictatorships. The Communist government had wanted to close the shipyard down, as Mrs Thatcher's administration might well have done if it were a British nationalized lame duck. The newly-elected government decided to privatize it, turning it into a public company with shares held by investors and workers alike.

Lured by the dream of a new dawn in her homeland, with a revitalized, rich economy, Barbara Piasecka-Johnson, a Polish-born American millionairess, and heir to the Johnson & Johnson fortune, set about establishing a joint venture with the trades union Solidarity to save the shipyard. It was fairly clear to just about everyone but Mrs Piasecka-Johnson and the Gdansk workforce that the idea was misconceived. Faced with job losses and a no-strike clause, the men from Solidarity saw the lady not as their saviour but as a major threat, and rejected her offer claiming she was trying to buy the yard on the cheap. Mrs Piasecka-Johnson retreated across the Atlantic, saying she wanted to make the yard profitable, not to buy it, and that

Solidarity did 'not know the meaning of the term "joint-venture"'.

I am sceptical as to whether corporatization will work. I tend to prefer a variation on the solution used by Henry VIII, when he wanted to abolish the Catholic church irreversibly: by giving away its property to anyone who mattered, he stripped it of its power.

In Eastern Europe, where the people have no savings of any substance for investment, why not hand over ownership of state enterprises to the people: after all they were supposed to belong to the people? If, then, they are found to have a real value, investors will come along and offer a market price, leaving the shareholders to decide whether to take cash or retain an investment. This concept was well argued by Professor Oliver Blanchard and Professor Richard Layard in an essay on Eastern Europe published in July 1990 by the Centre for Research into Communist Economics, which laid out a means of achieving the object of fair public ownership without resort to investment bankers, stockbrokers and public relations people.

The essay said that:

Fairness requires that every citizen be given a share in every enterprise. This can only be done through holding companies. Enterprises should be grouped into, say, five holding companies, and every citizen be given shares in every holding company. These shares would be traded and the daily publication of the holding company's price would put pressure on the holding company's managers to secure the best use of the capital which they controlled. The manager's pay would also be performance-based.

But the holding companies should not last for ever. Their job would be to reorganize their enterprises, establishing efficient management, and then progressively sell them off over a ten year period – distributing the proceeds to the shareholders. Since citizens would now own substantial private wealth (in holding company shares), there should be no difficulty in finding buyers for the reorganized enterprises, willing to buy at the right time.

One objection to this method is that 'people ought not to get something for nothing'. But, as Blanchard and Layard point out, the people have paid for most Eastern European capital anyway, through past taxation. It belongs to them, not to the politicians.

Some people have argued that shares should be given to the workers in enterprises. This would not be fair, since it would fail to reward other members of society who have made a contribution – such as teachers, nurses, doctors and those in genuine public employment.

In Britain, the government effectively made a gift of council houses and apartments to residents by selling them far below market value. In Eastern Europe, it would be just reward for years of subjugation for every man, woman and child to be given shares in the institutions they financed.

· 21 ·

Halfway house

MANY GOVERNMENTS, ESPECIALLY those of leftist leanings, fought shy of selling off state assets to members of the public, believing that they were serving the people's best interest by retaining ownership on their behalf.

There is some merit in the argument. Even those individuals buying shares in privatized state concerns will wish to sell them sooner or later. Upon the death of the shareholders, the shares will be passed on to heirs who may have no interest in either the investment or the enterprise. The chances are – and this has already been borne out by studies of the pattern of share ownership in British Telecom – that privately-owned holdings will be purchased by the big investment institutions. So, why should governments not retain ownership but at the same time attempt to run their enterprises as efficiently as the private sector?

This process has become known by another word – equally as ugly as privatization – 'corporatization'. Corporatization involves the transfer of public sector assets, usually from a government department, or a quasi-government institution, into a company structure, usually operating on commercial lines.

Its proponents argue that this permits bureaucratic administration to be replaced by commercial management, thus distancing the enterprise from undue political influence. They also believe that it allows centralized production-oriented decisions to be replaced by consumer and market-driven ones, while also allowing the introduction of clear performance targets.

This process has been tried, with some success, in Britain. Prior to their privatization, both British Airways and British Steel were partly liberated from Whitehall control, though the Government maintained a stranglehold on corporate borrowing and capital purchases. But it is to the Southern Hemisphere where we should turn for the most determined implementation of this strategy. New Zealand was the principal advocate of corporatization, keeping ownership of institutions within state control, but running them as private businesses. But it proved a halfway house, and such a poor alternative to privatization proper that it does not really merit further consideration.

· 22 ·

Selling the family home and the wireless

'The traditional European "public service" broadcasting organizations can expect to see their hegemony of the air waves rapidly eroded over the next decade'
– Andrew Neil, editor of the *Sunday Times*

'The word "conservative" is now used by the BBC as a portmanteau word of abuse for anyone whose political views differ from the insufferable, smug, sanctimonious, naïve, guilt-ridden, wet, pink orthodoxy of that sunset home of the third-rate minds of the third-rate decade, the 1960s'
– Norman Tebbit, Conservative MP and former minister in the Thatcher Government.

BY NO MEANS all of Thatcher's privatization programme was carried out by disposing of former government-owned assets to the private sector through the issue of equity to institutions and individuals. Indeed, although this method raised more money for the Exchequer than any other source, other forms of less-publicized privatizations continued apace.

Outside the equity issue, the biggest sell-off was of housing formerly owned by local authorities. In the first decade of privatization, more than 1.2 million local authority dwellings had been sold off for a total of £5,500 million. The council house or flat, once thought of as the preserve of the ne'r do well lower classes, was quickly transformed overnight into a highly desirable residence – especially if it was well-sited in a fashionable London borough like Westminster, Kensington and Chelsea, the City of London or Camden.

Those fortunate enough to occupy such habitats suddenly found not only that they could buy their homes at a substantial discount to market value, with mortgages freely available, but also that their newly-acquired assets suddenly shot up in value.

Following the publication in 1990 of the Audit Commission's controversial report, *Managing the Crisis in Council Housing*, the Government also sought to revive the concept of the private landlord. In Britain, private rental of inexpensive housing had all but been wiped out by the Rent Act, which gives tenants such a degree of protection that it is virtually impossible to shift them, even if you want to get back into your own home.

One method deployed was the Business Expansion Scheme (BES). Individuals who invested in companies providing housing for rent under an assured tenancy (despite its nomenclature, this meant one where you could ask a tenant to leave after the end of the lease) could get a 100 per cent tax rebate on their investment, provided they left it in for five years. For a while, there was a rash of BES property developments; the most popular being apartments for upwardly mobile young people, or yuppies, or retirement villages for the over 70s. These schemes continue, but have not attracted the popularity intended for them, partly because of the downturn in the property cycle, but also because some of the building companies behind them have found themselves in financial difficulties.

A more controversial plan was that of offering council tenants a choice of landlord: if a majority of tenants in a block of flats or on an estate agreed to have their properties come under the wing of a housing association, they could do so. The Housing Corporation, which has traditionally provided most of the funding for housing associations, suddenly found itself with £1.3 billion to spend instead of the usual £750 million, and able to almost double its construction programme. Housing associations were also encouraged to use mixed funding, with one-quarter of their funds coming from the private sector. Finally, councils were urged to turn to building societies and banks for funds.

THE LIBERATION OF BROADCASTING

Other assets once thought of as the exclusive preserve of government and the public sector were also put into play, the most visible of these being broadcasting.

One piece of legislation in 1984 set the scene for profound changes in television, and the Broadcasting Act of 1990 followed this through with a form of deregulation which spells the end of Reithian-type public broadcasting. Although significant changes in the way the British Broadcasting Corporation operates are unlikely before the BBC's charter expires in 1996, its power base and its dominant role are already being eroded. It is already no longer the significant organization it once was, and this is partly, though not entirely, due to the Thatcher Government.

The first legislation pushed through by Thatcher was seen as having little potential impact on the BBC, though in fact it did create the climate for change. This was the 1984 Cable and Broadcasting Act, which deregulated the fledgling cable television industry, and established the Cable Television Authority as the body to award franchises to operators who wished to dig up the streets in the towns and cities of Britain and lay cables through which television channels competing with the BBC–ITV duopoly could be relayed. The Cable Television Authority was told to regulate with 'a light touch' because, erroneously, it was seen as different from mainstream broadcasting – rather as a form of electronic publishing. There was much talk of local programming and home shopping from your television set.

The Cable Television Authority began its task with considerable energy, and was foolish enough to say it would be awarding five new franchises every four months. In practice, the capital investment required was so high that it was years before any substantial cable networks were established. Even six years

later, in 1990, only 350,000 households in Britain were con-
nected to cable, compared with over 25 million in the European
Community. Among the principal investors were water companies, who saw the benefit of laying coaxial cables alongside
the water mains which now reach almost every home in the
country.

But in 1990 the competition to terrestrial broadcasters from
cable hotted up, with more than two-dozen alternative channels
becoming available, ranging from the all-news Cable News
Network from the United States to two all-sport channels.
British Satellite Broadcasting (BSB) provided five networks of
films, entertainment and sport, while Rupert Murdoch's Sky
offered a further three, including one dedicated to movies and
another to news. The news programmes of CNN and Sky
became highly competitive with those of BBC and ITV –
especially at weekends when the terrestrial broadcasters opted
for short and inadequate bulletins.

By this time, both Sky and BSB – together with a range of
competitors from Europe – were also able to reach Britons'
homes through direct-broadcast satellites beamed at small
dishes which could be fixed simply to a roof or wall. These
satellite broadcasts were virtually unregulated, and although
most operators observed the normal standards of decency and
taste, others provided an almost non-stop supply of either pop
videos or erotica.

The established commercial broadcasters – companies like
Thames, Granada, Anglia, TVS and Yorkshire – were not
unduly troubled by the prospect of this new competition until
the Government decided to change the rules that had governed
Independent Television since its launch. Thatcher decided to
abolish the governing body, the Independent Broadcasting
Authority, seen as too heavy-handed, and to replace it with a
body with a lighter touch. More important, her cabinet agreed
that those licensed to broadcast on the mainstream national
commercial network, now known as Channel Three, should
have to compete in an open tender for the right to own a licence.

Until this point, licences had been awarded under an old-boy
network to those considered 'fit and proper' to run a television

company. In coming to a decision, the IBA was obliged to have regard for the programme plans and policies of a television company, as well as making an assessment of its financial strength and its ability to carry its plans out. The IBA had the right to withdraw licences from companies who failed to deliver on their promises, but it never did so, even though the approach of the five-yearly licence round was marked by a burst of ambitious programming and pledges of an equally ambitious schedule in the future. One licensee, TV AM, was reprimanded and warned by the IBA when its morning show fell far short of minimum standards, particularly of news and current affairs; but it was allowed to keep its licence.

The Thatcher Government rightly abolished the paternalistic IBA; but the system it introduced to replace it was regarded by some broadcasters and by the ITV companies with considerable dismay. By deciding to award licences to those who put in the highest tender, it was effectively privatizing a government asset: the airwaves. It was also deciding that wealth in abundance should be the principal yardstick by which the suitability of potential licence-holders should be judged.

David Mellor, the Home Office minister responsible for broadcasting, was adamant that, in contrast with the past, the incumbent ITV companies would not have a headstart. 'If they are ordering doubles and trebles all round, then I think they are being bloody silly,' he said. 'A track record will be helpful in gaining credibility, but there is no way the system is tilted in the existing incumbents' favour.'

The anguished ITV companies, unsure whether their businesses would continue to exist, lobbied furiously, but to little avail. In their lobbying, some of them revealed alternative strategies that, in themselves, would ensure that television would never be the same. Richard Dunn, chairman of the ITV Association, and chief of Thames Television, warned that if Thames failed to win renewal of the London weekday franchise, it might not follow the normal gentlemanly approach of selling its facilities, video library and staff to the new licensee, but would consider obtaining a transponder on the Astra satellite and broadcasting its programmes from that to the cable and satellite audience.

The result, of course, if either Thames or any other unsuccessful large incumbent ITV company were to take this step, would be to greatly enhance the prospects for cable and satellite, thus in turn achieving one of the Government's aims: diversity of ownership in broadcasting and reduced power for the big networks.

Apart from raising money from selling the ITV franchises to the highest bidder, the Government also decided to dispose of the hardware of independent broadcasting – the television and radio transmitters of the doomed Independent Broadcasting Authority.

The Home Office appointed the leading international accountancy and consultancy firm Price Waterhouse to lead this particular sale, and received some unexpected advice: that it should sell the transmitters of the BBC as well, creating two competing, geographically divided companies in the private sector to operate transmission.

Surprisingly, after being at the receiving end of some staunch lobbying from the BBC, the Government rejected the idea, and so only the £50 million-a-year IBA business will be sold off, either by a trade sale or a management buyout. The IBA's research and development operations are likely to be thrown in with the package, and, to encourage the new owners to carry them on, a levy on the fees paid by those tendering for broadcast licences will probably be made over to them.

This will leave the BBC as the only part of broadcasting still in the public sector. So where does the BBC stand in all this? Will it, too, be privatized, and sold off to the highest bidder?

What few people know is that the BBC was once in private ownership. Until 1927, radio broadcasting was run by a regulated private monopoly, before being taken into public ownership because it was felt that competition would lead to bedlam on the airwaves. It was in the report of the Crawford Committee on broadcasting which recommended nationalization of radio broadcasting, and that, interestingly, we find the first use of the term 'public interest'.

The BBC is fortunate in that it is endowed with a Royal Charter, which gives it a good deal of independence from the government of the day, although that has not stopped successive administrations from attempting to interfere with its operations.

It now offers more than 14,000 hours of television each year, and nearly 170,000 hours of radio on its four domestic networks, as well as a wide range of English and other language services on BBC External Services, which are financed directly by the Foreign Office, and which has ruthlessly cut them back and run them down over recent years.

The BBC would like to see the Charter renewed and a continuation of the licence fee, but this is by no means certain. Unless the licence fee rises by substantially more than the rate of inflation, the revenue thus generated will not be sufficient to allow it to maintain existing services. There remains a possibility that the Government will require the Corporation to take advertising, although the BBC has resisted any such suggestions with ferocious lobbying.

The BBC maintains that the intrusion of commercialism would cause severe long-term damage, but this may not be true. Some other state-owned broadcasters take advertising without disastrous effects. The New Zealand Broadcasting Corporation and the Canadian Broadcasting Corporation are two examples.

The BBC has also tried to run encrypted services on BBC 2 at night. One experiment operated by British Medical Television was largely funded by commercials for drug companies, but it went into receivership because of lack of support.

Although the BBC protests it is against advertising and commercialism, it is not adverse to allowing commercial companies to contribute towards the cost of its programming. In the Spring of 1990, BBC 1 ran a series about British Airways, which amounted to hidden sponsorship, and was perhaps the best publicity the airline had received for years. This followed a documentary about a small airline, Suckling Airways, which contained not a line of critical commentary, and was blatant free publicity. BBC also permits widespread sponsorship of sport carried on television. All this has been carried out without harmful effects.

It is hard to see any logical reason why the BBC should be treated differently from other nationalized industries, especially when a large proportion of its programming consists either of imported soaps or repeats. If the Conservatives are returned to office in the next election, privatization of the Corporation in one form or another seems inevitable.

The BBC's tactic will be to resist attempts to take away any of its services, using the argument that it is only right that the national broadcaster should appeal to all tastes. Marmaduke Hussey, the chairman, and Michael Checkland, the director-general, point to the example of the Australian Broadcasting Corporation, where its limitation to one national television channel has put it in a position where it no longer has a major popular audience.

One solution popular in some Tory circles is for BBC Television to be split from BBC Radio, and for each service to be limited to one channel. Local radio would revert to the private sector, as would the mass-audience stations, Radio One and Radio Two. The BBC, so the theory goes, would be left with enough air-time to make programmes that it does well: news and current affairs, science, the arts and drama. However sane this may sound, it is unlikely to be accepted by the Corporation except in the last resort.

For the present moment, the BBC will continue to be a political football. Its news and current affairs departments are constantly at the centre of controversy, being frequently accused of left-wing bias by the Conservative cavalry, led by Norman Tebbit. Labour's campaign and communications director, Peter Mandelson, has voiced the party's concern that the BBC might bow to Government-inspired pressure and lose its editorial independence, claiming there had been a 'sustained and systematic attack on BBC journalism by the Conservatives'. Mr Mandelson clearly has a short memory: some of the greatest pressure in the BBC's history was applied by the Wilson Government. Harold Wilson was perpetually at loggerheads with the Corporation, even after a former Labour minister had been appointed to the chairmanship of the board of governors.

It would be better for the BBC and for broadcasting if it ceased to become such a behemoth, and privatization, at least in part, is probably the best future for it. But both Britain and the world have reason to be grateful to the BBC for the pleasure and information it has provided over the years. It is now perhaps too cumbersome a bureaucracy, and too concerned with protecting its own patch, to remain a dynamic force in the 90s.

· 23 ·

Other forms of
privatization

'Tax, tax, tax; spend, spend, spend; elect, elect, elect'
– Franklin Delano Roosevelt

*'In Wandsworth we see the apotheosis of a far-reaching political change,
which will influence the development of politics both locally and nationally'*
– David Lipsey, writer and sociologist

IN 1990, THE Thatcher Government introduced what many
believed was its most unpopular reform: the community charge,
or poll tax as it was more commonly known. Life-long Tory
diehards resigned from the party because of it, and for back-
benchers, in the lobbies and luncheon rooms at Westminster, it
was the major topic of conversation.

The poll tax was designed to serve two purposes. The first
was to replace an inefficient system of property tax, known as
rates, by one which was spread across all citizens, whether they
owned property or not. Only 18 million people paid rates: 35
million Britons face the poll tax.

But it is the other reason for introducing the poll tax that is
relevant to privatization, for the Government aimed to bring
high-spending local councils, whether Tory or Labour, to heel
by making them accountable to the voters. As one former

Conservative minister explained, 'it was designed to bring home to the public the profligacy of local authorities, and it's doing it with a vengeance'.

What the former minister had in mind was that local authorities which privatized services like garbage collection by putting them out to contract would be able to become more efficient and charge ratepayers less than those councils which maintained large pools of direct labour.

Many voters did not see it that way at all. Families living in over-crowded subsidized council houses, like the Says from Witney in Oxfordshire, the scene of a major Tory revolt, found themselves with a total poll tax bill of £2,400 a year compared with rates of £418.60 – not because of the local authority's overspending, but because they had four grown-up sons living at home.

Still, the poll tax revealed wide differences between authorities that had already taken steps to privatize their services and those who had not. Wandsworth, known as Mrs Thatcher's favourite borough for its commitment to Government policies, introduced a poll tax of only £148, the lowest in England. A couple of miles away in Dulwich, where the Prime Minister had invested in a retirement home, the tax was well over double that, at £390 a head. Dulwich is in the London borough of Southwark, one of the least efficient of Labour councils, and one that has consistently been firmly opposed to privatization. In next door Lambeth, the situation looked even worse, with a poll tax of £550.

With its low rate, Wandsworth was one of the few urban areas in Britain where there were no street riots or protests against the Thatcher poll tax. As a South London police superintendent preparing his force for a night of disturbance in a nearby borough commented about Wandsworth, 'the likelihood of arrests there is somewhere between nil and zero'.

Wandsworth, once a dreary and dilapidated South London borough notable only for its gasworks, a smelly brewery and a scrubby common, is the epitomy of privatization at work at local level.

When the Conservatives took control of the council, it was one of the worst boroughs, and it had the highest rates. Its council estates were particularly drab. Led by Paul Beresford, a lively dentist from New Zealand, the new council set about reform, and made use of Thatcher legislation to the full. It took advantage of the Government's housing legislation, enabling it to sell off council houses and flats. Those who bought found they had to pay only 50 per cent of the market value, and the council arranged the mortgage. Those tenants who doubted the wisdom of doing so had their minds made up by the borough increasing the rents substantially. Properties left empty for lack of suitable tenants were sold off to those residents in the district who could prove they were first-time buyers.

The policy fed success, at least when measured by wealth. The council estates were spruced up by owner-occupiers and a determined parks department. Values shot up, benefiting those who had taken the plunge. By 1990, average house prices in Wandsworth had risen to £98,600; in Labour Lambeth they were £87,200.

Wandsworth also made a feature of contracting out, copying the example of the United States and Canada where almost all non-revenue earning activities are carried out by contractors who compete for the right to undertake them. The main objective is to seek the most cost-effective delivery of a service, such as refuse collection or building maintenance or security, by inviting tenders. In some cases, the existing public sector department is able to compete for the business.

Contracting out is not new. Ever since 1981, councils have had to put out certain areas of public sector building and civil engineering to public tender. The Local Government Act of 1988 reinforced this by declaring that most other services, including maintenance of parks and vehicles, street cleaning and catering should be phased into the same system.

The potential benefits of contracting out are: reduced costs; fewer employee difficulties because of less union involvement; improved service standards; reduced central overheads; and the greater use of specialist expertise. There are disadvantages, too. Sometimes existing staffs have to be laid off, resulting in costly redundancy payments. The performance of the contractors has to be closely monitored, to make sure that they maintain standards and do not cut corners. There is a danger of public sector contractors forming cartels, which are illegal in the United States, but hard to police in monopoly-loving Britain. And there is always the risk of corruption: local authority councillors or officials taking bribes or other inducements from those anxious to win a lucrative contract.

Wandsworth provides solid evidence of contracting out at work. Refuse collectors in the borough remove between three and four times as much garbage as those working for the neighbouring Labour councils. The average cost of refuse collection in inner-London per resident in early 1990 was £17; in Wandsworth the figure is almost half that at £9. Much, but not all, of the saving is in labour: when 216 refuse collectors employed by the borough went on strike in 1982, it was found possible to replace them by 120 working for a private contractor. What has happened to workers in almost every other industry is equally applicable to dustmen; but some councils have not faced up to their responsibilities to those who pay the bills.

Though refuse collection has been the most visible of contracting-out measures – and the easiest to implement because few people want to work as council dustmen – there are many other instances of where it is effective. In the past ten years, Wandsworth has been able to allow private contractors to take over 17 different functions, including some of those of administration.

At the time of writing, Wandsworth's Beresford had privatized 17 services and sold 16,500 council properties to tenants. He claims competitive tendering has saved the local authority £6.5 million a year. Now he is planning to capitalize on the demise of the Inner London Education Authority by taking over the local schools – outside London, of course, already a borough matter. Cuts on educational spending – offering still more benefits to residents – are in the pipeline, much to the anger of Labour protesters, who argue that social services have already suffered from a financial squeeze. Beresford will have none of it: he believes that the ILEA wasted so much money that his council will end up doing more while spending less.

In 1990, the Wandsworth experiment was put to the test at local elections. While nationally there was a swing to Labour, the Conservatives in Wandsworth increased their majority from one to 35. David Lipsey reported in the *Sunday Correspondent*:

> You did not have to spend long outside a polling station to be sure that the Tories were going to win. Through the gates flocked the yuppies. And their faces conveyed how they would vote: grim, a little guilty, but determined, like business executives who are not happy at having to sack a member of their staff, but know that their own prospects depend on it.

This colourful piece of journalistic licence failed to grasp the basic fact that 'yuppies' – whoever they may be – only represented a minor proportion of the voters. Ordinary people like councils that are efficient and run low-cost services. They do not like bureaucrats: the fewer they have to deal with the better. Socialists like Lipsey argued that the Conservatives had applied population management as a key strategy towards municipal power, shunting the poor out of Wandsworth into neighbouring boroughs:

> Poor people would not vote Tory; so poor people must be encouraged to leave the borough. You sell off the housing. Poor people in rotten council flats have no choice of being rehoused in the borough. So, if and when they can, they move to less inhospitable climes – perhaps, over the border, to the Labour client state of Lambeth. Their votes move with them.

There could be an element of truth in this, though surprisingly little evidence has been produced to support it. The argument to the contrary is equally powerful. You would have to be very poor indeed – and almost certainly unemployed – not to be able to afford to purchase a heavily-discounted council property. Many of those who voted Tory were relatively poor former Labour voters who had done just that. And, at the time of the local elections, the shortage of labour in London was such that any Wandsworth resident unable to find a job was probably unemployable. The problem of the long-term unemployed and their families is a major social problem in Britain, and is at least as great in Labour boroughs as in those controlled by the Conservatives – and certainly has nothing to do with either privatization or the poll tax.

There have been many examples of the new local privatization policy working well in other parts of Britain, but perhaps the most interesting development has been in the West Country city of Bath, where employees of the local council organized a management buyout of many of the authority's direct labour organizations, and then successfully competed for business.

The birth of the Bath Contractor Services Group (BCSG) was far from easy, even though it was created out of a semi-autonomous unit previously run as a profit centre within the Bath City Council, with bonuses paid to all employees in the good years.

In 1988, it won a number of building contracts under competitive tender, but the City revoked them because the prices were over the budget. At re-tender it won some of the contracts again, but found itself making less than 5 per cent of a return on capital, the rate required for council services.

Faced with the probability of his unit being wound up, the general manager, Christopher Jenkyn, investigated the possibilities of a management buyout. He and two colleagues took out second mortgages on their homes to raise equity of £90,000 and forwarded a business plan to Lloyds Bank's chief manager in Bristol, successfully persuading the bank to provide almost £750,000 in working capital.

The business plan was cautious and prudent, and forecasted sales of £3.5 million for the first year, compared with £4.2 million when the unit was under the control of the Bath City Council. The new company started with few assets, leasing existing equipment from the Council.

The employees were allowed two representatives on the board, and to own collectively 15 per cent of the equity, a concept which won the support of their unions who continued to be recognized for the purposes of collective bargaining. The area official of the Electrical, Electronic, Plumbing & Telecommunications Union, the main union, supported the plan because he saw it as the only way to protect jobs, and as a pioneer for national schemes.

In its first year, BCSG was meeting its targets – by seeking work beyond Bath as well as providing the City Council with services ranging from a 24-hour, 365-days-a-year emergency call-out support for council house owners to gardening and care of 400,000 plants in the city's parks and public places. It was also looking towards an investment in other direct labour organization management buyouts, and is working with its own advisers, Price Waterhouse, on advising others on how to carry them out.

In his new role Jenkyn seems like a happy man. But he said at the time: 'I'm not doing this because I want to. I would have been happy to remain a local authority employee for the rest of my life, but there is no future in it.'

· 24 ·

What's next for privatization?

'Our only problems are those of success'
– Sir Robert Reid, former chairman of British Rail

ACROSS THE WORLD, railways remain stubbornly resistant to privatization. Only in very few countries, such as the United States, are passenger rail networks in private hands, and even there the corporations who own them receive very large state and federal subsidies.

Privatized-rail in America no longer runs under romantic names. Gone are the great days of the Santa Fe Railroad, or the Long Island and Newhaven Line. The biggest rail company in the United States is just plain Amtrak, and it survives because businesspeople find the service it offers along the crowded North-East corridor of America marginally less unreliable than the delay-prone airline shuttles. It also receives huge annual subsidies from the American government, though these have fallen from $896 million in 1981 to just over $600 million in 1989. The Bush administration wants these cut to zero in 1991, but there is no chance of this happening.

Economists have been unable to explain why it is that very few railways are run at a profit. Even the Germans, who, with the Swiss, enjoy the best reputation for running services on time, manage to lose huge amounts of money in doing so. The more crowded, the more expensive the services – such as the London Underground – the bigger the losses.

Failure to make profits has not diminished governments' love affair with the train. The French have displayed the greatest passion for technological development with the introduction of the 185-miles-an-hour TGV express that whips businesspeople and tourists between Paris and Lyons in just two hours, and will soon speed passengers from Calais to the Bay of Biscay. The train is significantly faster than the plane. State-owned SCNF of France uses modern computerized booking and yield management systems. Fares are cheap, and competitive with air and road. In France, it truly is the age of the train. In 1990, SCNF introduced a new train operating safely at 340 miles an hour, breaking the world land speed record.

By contrast with the rail networks of Europe or Japan, railways in Britain, the pioneer of rail, are decrepit. Although clustered under a management monolith, British Rail, there is a total lack of uniformity of either standards of service or equipment. In the south-east sector of the country, rolling stock is electrically-powered by a shoe making contact with a live third rail – a dangerous system which would be banned by any sensible safety regulator. By contrast, most trains to the west of England – not the industrial heartland of the country – are the safest and fastest: high-speed diesels which cruise at 125 miles an hour. The rest of Britain is served either by electric trains powered by overhead lines or by old-fashioned, slow and inefficient diesels. In East Anglia, the fastest-growing part of Britain and the closest to the epicentre of the European Community, the railway services are at the worst and most unreliable, averaging little over 45 miles an hour even on express routes. Freight, where on the rails at all, moves even slower.

The state of British Rail is, inevitably, a favourite topic for those who write letters to newspapers, many of whom believe it beyond salvation. Even Mrs Thatcher makes known her distaste for travelling by rail, and although there is a fully-equipped resplendent Royal train, it spends most of its time idle in sidings and the subject of equally idle press gossip. The causes of British Rail's many failures are not a subject for debate in this

book: lack of investment and a succession of dreadful managements, particularly in the middle- to upper-layers, are among
them.

But if Mrs Thatcher shows little enthusiasm for journeying
by train, even when convention invites, there is no evidence that
she will shrink from including British Rail in the future privatization programme. On the contrary, the Thatcher Government's attitude towards British Rail in the latter part of the 80s
has provided every indication that it is being fattened up, like
the Christmas turkey, for privatization. It seems that only defeat
at the polls for the Conservatives stands in the way of rail
privatization.

But, to use an Americanism, turkey it is. There is very little
chance of the financial prospects of British Rail being significantly improved by the kind of deal the Government offered the
water authorities: a mixture of debt write-offs and a 'green
dowry'. For a start, the railways are labour-intensive, and
although many thousands of jobs have been lost in recent years,
and many thousands more will have to disappear, British Rail
will still need to remain a major employer in a very large service
industry. Just retraining the workforce, as the privatized British
Airways did, to inculcate management and labour to the belief
that they are there to provide a service, will be a costly
endeavour.

DECIDING HOW TO DO IT

Deciding that the railways should be privatized is, of course,
only the first, and easiest, decision. Deciding which way to do it
calls for much finer judgement.

At the start of the 90s, the Government was officially considering six options for the future of British Rail:

Privatizing the railways as a single network, along the
lines of the British Telecom, British Gas and British
Airways flotations.

Establishing a national track authority that would lease track time to competing companies, which might be national or regional in character.

Breaking up British Rail into its five existing business sectors: InterCity, Network SouthEast, Railfreight, Parcels and Provincial.

Recreating the pre-Second World War system of vertically integrated regional companies, each of which would operate a full range of services.

A hybrid solution combining elements of these four proposals.

Leaving British Rail as it is, thereby implicitly recognizing its social role as the provider of essential transport services.

Since this last option is thought to be not an option for a Conservative government, railway chiefs have already marshalled their public relations men and other lobbyists to argue for the first option, which at least would retain something like the status quo: in other words, that British Rail should be privatized as a whole and organized, as at present, in operating divisions. Under this arrangement, the existing management would presumably keep their jobs, and follow the example of executives in other privatized state industries in being much better paid. The trades unions are against privatization, but they, too, favour this choice if it is forced upon them.

They certainly do not favour the approach of privatization by segmenting the railways into business divisions, and they are joined in their implacable opposition to this by those who yearn for a return to the 'good old days' when the railways of Britain consisted of a number of fine and proud companies, each with their own virtues and liveries. There was the Great Western Railway, which operated its yellow and brown carriages out of Paddington with an unmatched quality of steam locomotives on its long haul routes. Meanwhile, the London Midland and Scottish Railway ran trains to the Midlands, the North-West and Scotland from Euston.

The London and North-Eastern Railway, spreading out north

from Kings Cross and east from Liverpool Street, broke world speed records for passenger trains with its famous engines, like the streamlined *Mallard*, a sight to set the pulses racing of schoolboy train-spotters as they watched it, whistle shrieking, steam billowing to the skies, haul the *Flying Scotsman* out of the tunnels near Barnet and into the Hertfordshire countryside.

The circle was completed with the less illustrious Southern Railway, but even it ran an efficient commuter service to Kent, Surrey and Sussex, and could boast the internationally-famous *Golden Arrow* to Paris, and the all-pullman trains *Brighton Belle* and *Bournemouth Belle*. These provided first class travel in every sense of the word; the *Brighton Belle* was famous for its regular clientele of actors and other theatricals who lived on the South Coast, and who used to enjoy their late-nightly supper trip home. Now, in the 90s, most of the services on routes from London to Brighton or Canterbury or Cambridge take longer than they did in the age of steam.

All this, said the traditionalists, could be created again, restoring the railways to their former glory, a view which was thought to be shared by the former Transport Minister, Paul Channon, who actually spoke publicly of a return to 'the good old days of the Great Western Railway and the LNER'. It turned out that this comment was said with heavy irony, for the pre-nationalization age was far from a golden age: all too often the rail services were slow, unreliable and infrequent, and the railway companies paid poor dividends to their unhappy shareholders.

The Government believes that nostalgia is no way to run a modern enterprise. It may work for the *Orient Express*, but not for a profit-making modern rail system. For a start, all the former private rail companies had their routes fanning out from London, unsuited to a modern industrialized Britain, where fast links from the centres of industry to mainland Europe are critical. The old LNER and LMS just would not be equipped to provide fast freight trains from Birmingham to Felixstowe, or high-speed passenger services from Bristol to Paris.

Fragmentation would also destroy the benefits of a network, which increases passenger demand by the provision of feeder services. Since British Rail has only about 7 per cent of the British passenger market – and only a slightly higher proportion of freight traffic – five small companies would end up with heavy overheads and only about 2 per cent each at best.

But the major objection to restoring the pre-nationalization system is that it would not increase competition. In each of the areas they served, the old companies constituted a private monopoly: why would the Government wish to replace British Rail with a series of private monopolies?

The most radical suggestion for privatizing British Rail – and the one feared by the railway chiefs – is the one likely not only to produce profits, but also to improve services to the passenger, or customer.

This involves selling off the track, together with the signalling and the stations, to something like a 'National Track Authority', which would then lease out use of the lines and stations to private operators. This has several advantages. It enables the national interest to be preserved in decisions as to which tracks should be maintained or closed, or indeed reopened. It provides for proper competition in the provision of rail services. It allows the Government, through the use of its golden share, to impose stringent safety standards upon both the Authority and also those who rent its tracks. British Rail has proved itself to be one of the world's least safe railway systems: anyone who doubts that this was the fault of management under Sir Robert Reid's leadership should read the official report on the Clapham Junction rail disaster of 1989.

The report revealed that technicians had been working on the signalling seven days a week because there were not enough skilled employees to do the work. One reason for this was the poor rates of pay offered to skilled staff in the South East: the British Rail management had consistently given in to the unions who have consistently opposed attempts to provide regional variations in pay.

One way the track authority scheme could work was suggested by John Redwood, a former head of the Downing Street Policy Unit, who advocated leasing the lines to regional companies and separating companies running freight and InterCity.

This seems to me a poor half-way house. Why not allow private companies to tender for competitive services on the same tracks? And the National Track Authority could, itself, be a privatized body. It would, in fact, occupy a similar role to the British Airports Authority and the Civil Aviation Authority. While the BAA has its critics for its insatiable desire to turn London's Heathrow and Gatwick Airports into suburban shopping malls, they are infinitely more attractive places to wait for a delayed flight than, say, Hamburg, Frankfurt or Charles de Gaulle in Paris. And they make money!

This means of privatization had the support of the former Transport Secretary, Paul Channon. In a paper on privatization published in 1989, he wrote:

> The advantage of the track company is the potential for introducing competition in the provision of train services. The main consideration here is how far it would be possible to achieve real competition, given the constraints of railway operation, which has the need for complex timetabling for safety reasons.

British Rail's management does not like the idea, and it argues it has enough competition from the roads without having to organize it on the rails. But that is mainly because as a management it is steeped in outmoded attitudes. As a nationalized concern, British Rail has had an ambivalent attitude towards the conduct of commercial enterprise on railway property. At London termini it has been encouraged, even privatized, but out of town it has been rather frowned upon. On most provincial stations, the best the passenger (customer) can expect is a rather poorly-provided magazine stall, more often than not shut, and one of those really dreadful Travellers Fare cafes where both the sandwiches and the sausage rolls give the impression of having been marinaded in sawdust.

There is no reason why railway stations should not become worthwhile retail centres, as indeed they have become in Japan. Even in minor European cities, one can rely on getting a good meal at the Café de la Gare, while in the United States one of the most successful restaurant chains is Victoria Station, which prides itself on recreating rail stations as they used to be in the good old days. Even in Britain such places exist: at Elsenham Station in Essex, the old carriages of the *Brighton Belle* marshalled in a convenient siding provide a good local eaterie.

Having established a track authority, this body could then invite tenders from those who wish to run services along them. This is not as complicated as it sounds – and certainly no more complex than deciding who should be permitted to fly air services from London to Paris. Generally, the same rules could apply: on major routes there could be several service providers; on most routes there would have to be at least two; and monopolies would only be permitted on branch lines deemed only marginal. As with privatized bus services, those seeking the right to provide rail travel would have to offer to run trains at unsocial hours as well as at peak periods.

Thereafter, those given licences would be free to offer the quality of travel and pricing they felt most suitable. They also would be free to employ their own labour, regardless of the whims of the National Union of Railwaymen (NUR) or ASLEF, two unions who seem to have been allowed to continue to throttle their industry long after the brethren in other sectors have given up.

There would be premium expresses and slow trains. First class would mean first class, with newspapers and croissants and coffee provided in the early morning. Most trains covering trips of over 45 minutes would offer refreshments served at the seat. Restaurant cars, after timekeeping perhaps the biggest single indictment of British Rail under Sir Robert Reid, would offer varied fare. It has never ceased to amaze me that whereas in the small East Anglian village in which I live, it is possible to get an Indian, Chinese, French or fish and chip meal at almost any hour, the only hot food on the buffet car on the overcrowded trains to Cambridge consists of microwaved bacon burgers and stale sausage rolls. On the 8.20am from Audley End to Liverpool Street, the guard frequently announces that due to boiler failure there 'is no tea or coffee this morning, but a fine selection of beers, wines and spirits is available'.

Under a well-privatized railway system, good trains would gain a reputation as such, and would become sought after. And if the National Track Authority failed to maintain the signals or the points, it would soon hear about it from the Fen Railway Company or the Cambridge Express Group, or perhaps the Brighton Belle Ltd.

Sir Robert Reid, who has been a railwayman for almost as long as the railways have been a dismal failure, would no doubt reject this concept as utopian, but one has only to visit socialist Sweden to find that such things are possible. Each morning a businessperson's train leaves Linchoeping for Stockholm: each customer has their own desk, telephone and portable computer, as well as the use of a fax, and a coffee and croissant if he or she wishes. As with BR's Pullman trains, a surcharge is made for travel on such trains.

At the time of writing, it seems unlikely that British Rail will become an early candidate for privatization, partly because of the difficulties already explained, but mainly because it is in a totally different category to private monopolies like British Telecom, British Gas and the new water companies. British Rail has to compete with the heavily-subsidized private road sector, where the road-haulage industry pays nowhere near its appropriate contribution to the infrastructure the Government provides for it.

British Rail may, of late, have been set commercial targets, but it has only moved some way towards achieving them through asset sales of valuable railway land, or by massive city centre development projects, such as the rebuilding of Liverpool Street Station, where most of the space has been turned over to high-price City offices.

As ministers' thoughts turn towards elections and the need to revive waning Conservative popularity, price-rises British Rail chiefs deemed necessary have been rejected by the Government, which has also forced an effective incomes policy on rail staff. Intervention by a variety of ministers has inhibited British Rail's management.

Many people argue that removing the politician from the driver's seat in British Rail will be the single most effective step in making the railways more efficient. The nationalized railways have been a political football for more than four decades, and privatization is the only answer. Whichever way they are privatized, the new companies should be free to pay both staff and management according to their skills and location, rather than under outmoded and outdated agreements. The pay of railway workers will go up, but their numbers will go down. The person to tackle the daunting task of remodelling the railways is Sir Colin Marshall, chief executive of British Airways. But, if I were him, I would not want the job.

RAIL VERSUS ROADS

Properly organized, there is little danger of the railways obtaining the monopoly power endemic to many of the British Government's other privatizations, like British Gas and British Telecom.

The toughest competition for a privatized rail network will not come from within its own framework, but from the roads. At present, the railways have less than one-eighth of the market for passengers or freight, and although a more efficient privatized system will improve on this, it is unlikely to find itself in a position where it will be able to threaten road transport, except in heavy commuter populations like Greater London – and this is likely to be considered environmentally desirable. Medium-distance routes are more cheaply and efficiently served by coach: the cost of a round trip from Norwich to Central London by fast coach is less than one-third of the comparable rail journey and just as quick when London connections are taken into account. On long haul routes the train is superior in time to the coach, though much more expensive, but here the railways are beaten hands-down by airlines, especially on cross-country trips avoiding London. This is not so true in Western Europe, but that is a different story. The British taste for public transport has faded along with its declining standards of comfort and safety.

But if roads offer stiff competition, they can hardly be

presented as a fine example of free enterprise, as the powerful road transport lobby would have us believe. In fact they are even less privatized than today's British Rail or other forms of public transport. Between 1982 and 1989, public expenditure on roads, car parks and cars, including the tax subsidy on company cars, came to more than £33 billion: in this period, spending on public transport was less than £20 billion. The cost of supporting the private car is, of course, much greater than the figures suggest: for they do not take into account the cost of accidents, police patrols and damaging the environment. In Britain, the car is responsible for one-fifth of Britain's carbon dioxide emissions, about two-fifths of the contribution to acid rain, and almost all the lead in the atmosphere, which damages children's brains, particularly those whose primary schools abut such grimy highways as London's South Circular Road.

Britain's roads are not privatized, either in ownership or in the way they are run. They are funded and operated almost entirely by the state out of government funds. Compared with socialist France, which has a nationwide network of expensive toll roads paid for, as should be the case, by the most frequent users, or Switzerland, which levies all those who want to drive on its autoroutes a fee of £15 a year, Britain has almost no toll roads. Most are anachronisms. There is the Dartford Tunnel, which costs motorists 70 pence for the one mile trip. Why penalize drivers using the east side of the M25 as against the busier west? Why not adopt the Swiss system requiring all motorists using this and other overcrowded roads to buy a green sticker? At the other extreme there is the Dulwich toll gate, which levies a modest ten pence on those taking a short cut down the College's private road.

The result of this illogical attitude from a government supposedly dedicated to free enterprise is that most motorists pay significantly more for keeping their vehicles stationary – in expensive garages or in the well-priced car parks of another unloved government-permitted monopoly, National Car Parks – than they do in the right to use the roads.

If the motorway system was truly privatized, then those who use them would pay an economic price for driving on them, and would be able to buy shares in the companies that owned and operated them. These companies would be under both a statutory and a social obligation to maintain the motorways in good condition, and ensure high safety standards, including full lighting. The kind of poorly-organized contraflows endemic on the M1 and the M25 – and a contributory factor to so many serious accidents involving loss of life and disablement – would be replaced by the well-supervised French system of handling autoroute repairs. Owners of motorways would be liable for accidents caused by the part-negligence of their employees. Motorway owners would also be obliged to install high technology ensuring that those breaking speed-limits or committing other traffic violations can be caught and fined before leaving the route.

In return, the motorway owners would get the rights to the tolls for a substantial number of years, with inflation-proofing provided by the introduction of some kind of K-factor, as used in the case of British Telecom and British Gas. There would, of course, be argument over the length of the period. Eurotunnel has a 55-year concession to operate the Channel Tunnel, a rail-only link. BICC, the construction and cables group, failed to win the second Severn Bridge crossing because it wanted more than 23 years to reduce the toll below £1.30; John Laing won the deal by offering £1.20 for three years, rising to £1.40 thereafter.

But this kind of thing is anathema to those self-presumed champions of free enterprise, the British Road Federation (BRF), which wants more government money for more taxpayer-supported roads, argues for heavier lorries operating under less stringent controls, and seeks for a reduction in vehicle taxation. Other lobbyists for the roads include the Royal Automobile Club (RAC), which seeks higher speed limits and other relaxations, irrespective of the damage likely to be caused. The RAC would, of course, be the first to protest if the City of Westminster decided to permit the construction of a helipad at the rear of its sumptuous club in Pall Mall. The BRF – together with the RAC and the Automobile Association – have powerful friends at Westminster. The BRF finances the All Party Road

Study Group, which is run from the offices of a public relations firm, Charles Barker, and regularly lobbies civil servants and ministers against privatization and user-pay schemes.

Their lobbying has been successful, and Mrs Thatcher shows no inclination to extend the principle of user-pay – favoured for the health service, the universities, local government and a range of other government-provided facilities – to motorway finance. And unless that happens, which company in its right mind is likely to finance a trunk route, knowing that motorists and hauliers who use it will rightly protest that in one part of the country they are likely to have to pay heavily for something they 'are used to getting for nothing'?

That is why *New Roads by New Means*, the Government's 1989 green paper on road transport, was a flop. A mixture of flawed logic and the kind of Victorian nostalgia articulated by the Prime Minister, it expressed the hope that 'entrepreneurs with the imagination and initiative of Brunel', the nineteenth-century engineer and railway builder, would come out of the woodwork and identify new roads and river crossings that could be built to achieve the twin objective of alleviating congestion and providing their builders with a profit.

It does not take any great intellect to conclude that so long as the rest of the motorway network continues to be heavily subsidized, this will not work. One specific proposal was to extend the M11 with a privately-built motorway up the east side of Britain, from Cambridgeshire to Newcastle. No one was interested in building it, not surprsingly given that in all but the heaviest of conditions, most road users would opt for the free M1 from north Yorkshire to the M25, unless the tolls were set at such a low rate as to be unviable. Labour's transport spokesman, John Prescott, commented that the Government was trying to solve twentieth-century problems with nineteenth-century policies. He was right, except that *New Roads by New Means* was not a policy at all, but a classic Whitehall fudge, designed to introduce an element of privatization to a system that is a government-monopoly serving certain sectorial interests.

In the end, not one private-sector builder accepted the

Government's challenge to come up with a new route, and the Transport Secretary, Cecil Parkinson, was forced into a more modest tactic, inviting tenders to build toll roads in areas identified as where demand for a congestion-free route would be great. These included the Birmingham Northern Relief Road, and a second river crossing of the Lower Thames. But, with interest rates at record levels and inflation rising, there were few takers, and in the Spring of 1990 it looked as if Parkinson would have to find more taxpayers' money to subsidize their construction.

Meanwhile, at the other end of the world, in Malaysia, a privatized 867-kilometre north–south toll expressway linking the Singapore border in the south with Thailand in the north is being built. The method is the 'build–operate–transfer' system which gives the shareholders the concession to collect tolls for 30 years. Shareholders include the backbone of the multi-racial coalition, the United Malays National Organization. Schroder Wagg, from the City of London, was the adviser to Dr Mahathir Mohamad's government.

Perhaps we shall witness a Parliamentary delegation visiting Malaysia to tell us how they do it more effectively there?

· 25 ·
Privatized post?

ALMOST AS DIFFICULT to privatize as the railways are the postal services, partly for the same reason. The post offices of the world argue that they provide a social service, and that if their monopoly is taken away, then it will no longer be possible for them to provide deliveries and collections in remote rural areas.

Like the railways, too, post offices already face substantial competition. Many of their counter services are now replicated by the major banks and building societies – and if people have accounts with these institutions, they are more likely to use them than to queue at the post office. At the other end of the scale, international courier companies like the American DHL group or Australia's TNT offer guaranteed overnight delivery services of parcels and packets to almost anywhere in the world. These services are particularly popular with business because they tend to be more reliable and quicker than those of the post office.

On a smaller scale, each town and city in Europe has motor-cycle messengers – of which some are engaged by courier companies and some self-employed. They specialize in kami-kaze-style riding and fast delivery: if you want a package to be sent to anyone in London fast and reliably, you phone for a bike.

In countries like Britain the postal service, particularly for first-class mail, is also under intense challenge from facsimile transmission. Once you have bought a fax machine – and now even the smallest businesses have them – you can send a letter to anyone else who has a fax machine for less than a second-class stamp; and substantially less if you program your faxes to be sent at cheap rates during the night. The principal beneficiary in the fax business is privatized-British Telecom, but in many European countries post and telecommunications are still one and the same bureaucracy, maintaining a stranglehold on telecommunications.

It is unlikely that this stranglehold will last, and their fate will almost certainly be determined by the European Commission in Brussels, where officials are preparing a blueprint on the future of both postal services and telecommunications. The lobbying of Commission officials is already intense. The existing PTTs and post offices want to see their monopolies enforced and extended so as to outlaw private courier services. The courier companies want all monopolies in Europe scrapped, allowing free competition for the mails.

West Germany, France, Belgium and Italy have been the most determined to maintain their monopolies, and all have been told by the Commission to mend their ways and accept that they certainly cannot stop international courier services from operating. Some, especially the British and the Dutch, have sought to fight back against the private couriers with their own premium services. The British Post Office's Datapost boasts that it can out-compete anybody, anywhere.

So long as socialist governments dominate many parts of Europe, it is unlikely that post offices will neither lose their monopoly on private letters nor will they be privatized. But competition is likely to be introduced on all premium services, and once telecommunications are deregulated and use of the fax extends to all parts of Europe, it is hard to see much of a case for keeping the mails in the public sector. But there is not a place in the world where the post office is privatized, and it may be one of the last bastions of government activity to fall.

· 26 ·

Schools – public or private?

FEW SUBJECTS HAVE caused as much emotion in Britain as education. When education became compulsory after the Second World War, a national schools system was established in Britain to enable each child to be 'educated according to his or her needs'. Education was also free. From the age of five, children attended primary schools. At the age of ten or 11, they were tested in an examination. This selection process picked a minority for an academic education at a grammar school: the remainder were given what was billed as a broader-based education at secondary modern schools.

This process enabled a number of children from the working classes to access the universities, previously the preserve of those whose parents could afford to fund private education. But it also meant that a majority of children were given a second-rate education, and not surprisingly, one of the first acts of the Wilson Labour Government was to abolish selection at aged 11 and cause grammar and secondary modern schools to be merged into comprehensives. This was scarcely a radical step. Countries as varied as the United States and Scandinavia had long had non-selective schools.

But, at the same time as it introduced this move, the Labour Party also committed itself to abolishing private education. It was wrong, argued Labour, for the rich to be able to buy privilege in education: there should be equality of opportunity for everyone. Even counting up its own Cabinet ministers, most had only been able to get a university education because they had been to private schools like Eton, Harrow, Westminster or Charterhouse.

Labour was never able to carry this policy through, and over the years only the hard-left have maintained the commitment. By the time the Tories had returned to government in 1979, private education was seen as more desirable, more expensive and more liable to secure a child a better start in life than ever before.

Prime Minister Thatcher, herself a grammar-school girl and the product of the selective system, was the daughter of a small-town grocer, who would not have been able to afford to send young Margaret to a private school. She knew that had she been at one of Labour's comprehensive schools, the chances of her reaching Oxford University, and ultimately 10 Downing Street, would have been much reduced. As a former Education Secretary — her first senior ministry — she was also concerned about falling standards, particularly in the teaching profession.

But both she and her Education Ministers (Sir Keith Joseph and later Kenneth Baker) stopped short either of returning to selective education or of privatizing it. The Government tinkered with the idea of issuing education vouchers to parents, giving them the right to use them, like beads at a Club Mediterranean resort, to purchase schooling for their children at schools of their choice, including the private sector. But the idea dropped into the 'too hard' basket, not least because the best schools would be in the most demand, and vouchers would not deal with the problem of how to decide whose children should win a place at an establishment of their choice.

Now the problem is more seriously compounded by a loss of confidence between educators and parents, and between each of these groups and the Government. The Government genuinely wants to lift standards, but the changes it has made to the curriculum seem designed to achieve the opposite. For some extraordinary reason, it seems to be placing increased emphasis on religious education — while reducing science specialization just at a time when other countries are developing it. Teachers complain and believe Thatcherism means less money spent on schools. Parents are confused, but they do not like what they hear, and those that can afford to do so opt increasingly for thriving private schools. Even those well outside the top league can command annual boarding fees of £7,500 or more, and can take their pick of pupils from long waiting lists.

If ever there was an issue over which the Thatcher Government has lost its cutting edge, this is it. Privatization of the education system, offering genuine competition between schools, could provide the biggest single spurt to badly needed improved standards, which now lag behind those in the major industrialized nations.

It is indeed curious that a country that has led the world with high-quality private education should be afraid to extend this system to the nation as a whole. British private education is a success story – whether it be the nursery school in Kensington, direct-grant schools like St Paul's or the establishments of the Girls Public Day School Trust, independent schools like Winchester, Gresham's and Marlborough – which attract pupils from the world over – or post-graduate establishments like the London Business School. Most, if not all, of these institutions may be non-profit making, but they are privatized. They are run by independent boards of governors, not by politicians or public servants.

The role of the state in these bodies is as it should be. It sets the educational standards, which are, indeed, themselves privatized through the various examination bodies. Department of Education inspectors supplement parental bodies and boards of governors as an active watchdog over the schools. In the case of direct-grant schools, the Government makes a contribution towards their cost, and local authorities fund bursaries. But it does not appoint either the principals or the teachers, nor does it build or maintain buildings, run the catering, supply the books or audio-visual equipment and computers, or provide the administration.

Putting the rest of the education system on this footing would be a relatively simple task, especially now that the community charge, or poll tax, has become the foundation stone for financing local government, which has the task of running state schools. Each household with a child of school age would receive a grant sufficient to cover the cost of education as at present provided. At the end of the tax year, the responsible parent would have to prove that the grant has been spent at a certified education establishment – or it would be collected as taxation. Extras, such as school trips overseas, additional coaching and extra-curricular activities, would be funded by parents, by local donation or by the school governors selling the use of facilities to those who wish to use them. How many school tennis courts, swimming pools, playing fields, language laboratories and other facilities are left idle at weekends and in the holidays?

· 27 ·

Privatized tax gathering

BRITAIN, WITH ONE-FIFTH of the tax base of the United States, has the same number of tax officers. And that is not all. Britain also spends per pound two and a half times the cost of the operations of the inefficient Inland Revenue in the administration of the social security system – a staggering discrepancy given that the tax system applies to nearly everyone, while the social security system applies only to those in need.

Could it all be privatized?

There are undoubtedly some objections to the idea which even the most stoic supporters of Thatcherism would accept. People's incomes are a private matter between them and the tax inspector. Most individuals would baulk at their tax returns being seen by a third party, though of course employers know what their workers earn. Many individuals use accountants and other tax advisers as intermediaries between them and the revenue.

It is perhaps possible to conceive of a situation whereby private commissioners – like a Notary Public or a Justice of the Peace – are authorized to agree tax returns with those who wished to use them, thereby alleviating the burden on hard-pressed taxation offices: but it could be a cumbersome solution.

The answer, surely, is to make the collection of taxes and the management of social security more efficient within the public sector, and to use private enterprise where it is appropriate.

One of the greatest inefficiencies in the taxation of individuals is the coding system. It is also the system which imposes burdens on employers as well as government. Every time an individual's circumstances change – through marriage, divorce, the acquisition of a mortgage, old age or a variety of other factors such as the birth of a child – his or her code is altered and a piece of paper is sent to both individual and employer. The latter then begins to deduct tax at another rate. The purpose of the exercise is sensible: to be fair to the taxpayer by not deducting too much or too little tax each week so that at the end of the year an adjustment is unnecessary.

But the cost of this operation far outweighs its benefits, and most Western governments manage to do without it. In Australia and the United States, for example, everybody pays basic tax according to scale: at the end of the tax year, it is obligatory to complete a declaration within a matter of weeks. Since most people are entitled to rebates for allowances they may claim, returns are produced swiftly, and, in the case of Australia, the government undertakes to get the tax cheque in the post equally speedily.

· 28 ·

Are the Royals them or us?

'We must not let daylight in on magic'
– Walter Bagehot, on the need for dignity between Crown and people

'If there is no need for the state to mine coal, there is clearly no need for the state to keep palaces. The monarchy should be privatized'
– Brian Oxley, Conservative Party researcher

'IS THERE NO stopping that woman?' I heard a member of the gerontocracy mutter to a friend in the members' bar of the RAC Club. 'She will privatize the Royal Family next.'

The gentleman totally missed the point. The Saxe-Coburg-Gotha dynasty, now better known as the Windsors, has always been privatized. King George V used to call them the 'family firm', and that is exactly what it is. The difference from other firms or companies is that the Windsors have, like British Gas, been enjoying a state monopoly, but without a watchdog like OFGAS to report on their performance. To which the Duke of Edinburgh might well reply: 'With the *Sun* and the *Daily Mirror* on our tails every day, who needs a watchdog!'

The monarchy is, however, less privatized than it used to be. In medieval times the King was the state, collecting all taxes and dispersing all expenditure according to his whim and to the

· 182 ·

demands and pressures placed upon him. In Britain, not even the most avid Monarchist would wish to return the country to such a condition today, though there is no telling what some former monarchs will get up to in order to vanquish republicanism. For some time, King Constantine of Greece nursed a desire to reinstate the Athens monarchy, while the exiled King of Romania attempted unsuccessfully to return to Bucharest after the tyrannical Ceauseascus had been executed.

In Britain, talk of further privatization of the Royals is a nonsense, unless the concept is to abolish the present constitution and replace it with a republic, in which case there is no place for a monarch at all. In a republic, the Royals would become just like any other well-to-do family. In republican Germany and Italy, for instance, there are a number of personages who presume titles of count or baron and who claim their ancestry entitles them to do so. Some of them have emigrated to Australia, where they try to throw their weight about on the social scene.

Those who talk glibly about privatizing the Windsors rarely mean they wish to see the establishment of a republic, although there is some support for that. What they really are saying is that they would like the Windsors to stand more on their own feet, and receive less of a subsidy from the Exchequer for the public duties they perform. That is a different matter, and is an issue for public debate, just like subsidies for British Rail. The fact that it is not debated is an indication of the deference in which the Royal Family is still held, despite – perhaps because of – the escapades of its various members.

There is also very little point in debating the issue so long as Queen Elizabeth II refuses to disclose how much she and her family are worth. Estimates vary from £2 billion to six or seven times that amount. Nominating the Queen as Britain's richest person, the *Sunday Times* magazine said her portfolio of shares and bonds, estates, and works of art and jewellery were worth £1.2 billion.

Attempts have been made by both friends of the family and its critics to persuade the Royal Family to end the speculation over their worth, but to no avail. Even the House of Commons select committee on the civil list does not have this information. In the meantime, the amount voted by Parliament to the Queen for fulfilling the role of head of state and maintaining the royal household is currently over £6 million.

The obligation upon the Monarch to disclose wealth is a moral, not a legal, one. The Royals are exempt from taxation, so the normal obligation upon an individual to tell the Inland Revenue how much he or she is worth does not apply. Nor does the Monarch own the crown estates, as many people believe to be the case. They belong to the public. King George II surrendered these vast landholdings in 1760 in return for the civil list, and total relief from the previous Royal obligation to pay for the civil service and the diplomatic corps.

So long as we expect the Windsors to carry out public duties, the civil list must remain, but its use should perhaps be more strictly confined to the Royals' official, rather than their private, role. Is it really necessary for the civil list to cover the cost of so many palaces? Why should Prince Edward receive finance from the civil list when he rarely carries out public duties?

Apart from those properties provided and maintained for their use by the civil list, the Royals own vast landholdings in their own right, including the Duchy of Cornwall estates, the personal property of the Prince of Wales. An exception within the Royal Family, he uses the income from the Duchy to finance his own household, though not of course his official travels. This is praiseworthy, but it is not privatization because the property is already his.

Such further privatization of the Royals as is possible is limited to making more commercial or public use of the facilities already provided for their use by the civil list and the Exchequer. It may be impractical to use Royal Air Force aircraft of the Queen's Flight for commercial purposes – but there is certainly no need for the planes to be grounded for so much of the time. They could perhaps be available on private charter.

The Royal yacht *Britannia*, which costs the Government £6 million a year, could be moored in the Thames near the City of London and used as a conference centre when not transporting the Family in other parts of the world. The costs of hiring it, of course, would be heavy, but since the HMS *Belfast* is rented out at a profit for City cocktail parties, there seems no reason not to obtain some revenues from *Britannia* for marginal extra costs.

The possibility of charging those invited to parties also attended by the Royals has been considered: after all, that is what effectively happens at charity occasions. But it seems more sensible to use these occasions for commercial advantage by allowing industry and exporters to capitalize on the attraction.

My suggestion would be to persuade the Royals to vacate all but a small part of Buckingham Palace. The Queen and the Duke of Edinburgh spend very few nights there anyway, preferring the former hunting lodge at Windsor Great Park as a family home. Buckingham Palace and its grounds could then be converted into London's most expensive and sassy hotel.

· 29 ·
Conclusion

'Privatization has transformed a substantial sector of the British economy and brought about the largest extension of share ownership we have ever seen in Britain. The achievements give the lie to the accusation that the only reason for privatization was to raise money for the Exchequer'
– Nigel Lawson, former Chancellor of the Exchequer

'The basic shift is from central government to individual empowerment. From public housing to home ownership. From national health service to private options. From government regulation to market mechanisms. From welfare to workfare. From collectivism to individualism. From government monopoly to competitive enterprise. From state industries to privatized companies. From state industries to employee ownership. From tax burdens to tax reductions'
– American forecasters John Naisbitt and Patricia Aburdene, in their futuristic book, *Megatrends 2000*

'I am not able to say myself whether it will be worth all the labour involved in privatization. I do not know. I think we shall find out only a lot later on'
– Sir Denis Rooke, chairman of British Gas

MARGARET THATCHER, THE grocer's daughter, may not have buried Socialism, her defined ambition, but she has certainly rolled back the frontiers of state. When she swept into power in 1979, the nationalized industries accounted for about one-tenth of gross national product, and a seventh of total investment. By the end of the 80s, half of that was under private ownership. Privatization, a policy pursued most vigorously in Britain, is also becoming the global doctrine of the 90s.

From Brazil to Bangladesh they are swapping state industries for private industries. Even countries with socialist governments are pursuing privatization with vigour. Nigeria wants to sell the government stake in over 150 banks, insurance companies and breweries. Mozambique has privatized more than 20 industrial plants. Even one of the cosiest welfare states in Europe, the Netherlands, is at long last contemplating privatization.

But the real changes are most likely to be in Eastern Europe, in the countries that used to be known as the Soviet Bloc or the Warsaw Pact countries. Until 1989's peaceful revolution, almost all of industry in Poland, Hungary, Czechoslovakia and East Germany was in the hands of Communist-controlled governments.

Now the desire is to remove the power of the state, and the dead hand of the bureaucrats who were the *apparatchiks* of state enterprises. The 45 years of Communism that has produced a 12 million-long waiting list for telephones in the Soviet Union is in retreat.

The issue in many countries now is not whether to privatize, but how to do it. There is the question of what to sell. Is it only the profitable enterprises, or is it lame ducks as well, in the hope that private management will revitalize a moribund concern? There is the question of how to sell it – to extract the best price. And there is the issue of how to make sure the public interest, where appropriate, is still served.

Unfortunately the British, though the pioneers of privatization, have not excelled at it. Although the climate for introducing new competition for privatized enterprises could not have been better, the Thatcher Government has missed a wonderful opportunity. Instead of producing an airline policy that would have provided British Airways with true competition from its principal rival at the time, British Caledonian, Thatcher handed

Lord King a monopoly on a plate and allowed him to behave like a monopolist. Instead of breaking up the British Broadcasting Corporation into separate radio and television interests, the Government allowed it to retain a predominant position, although questions remain about its future in the 90s. Instead of introducing anti-competitive legislation of the kind that has trimmed monopolies in the United States, Thatcher persisted with a pedantic and inefficient Monopolies and Mergers Commission whose major thrust at times seemed to preserve traditional British industries from overseas takeover rather than promote genuine competition.

British Telecom, British Gas and the various privatized water boards are at least as powerful monopolies as they were in the state sector, with fewer controls or restraints on their activities. These giant monopolies also have shown little sense of adventure, preferring to exploit their cosy, government-given monopolies at home. Not for them the opportunities that exist for developing their businesses in Eastern Europe or Africa, regions that need caring capitalism more than anywhere else. Exploiting opportunities here has been left to businesses in socialist France or Italy, or to American or German companies.

It also seems to me that if the Conservatives had ideals in pursuing the policies of privatization, then ministers pursued them with such an eye on expediency that the principles were never properly applied. The first Conservative election manifesto of the 80s pledged that the Tories would not 'merely replace state monopolies by private ones as that would waste an historic opportunity to ensure that they do not exploit their position to the detriment of customers'. This promise has been cynically disregarded.

Perhaps this is unfair criticism? Perhaps it was not cynicism; perhaps ministers just gave in to the bureaucrats, who, in true *Yes Minister* style, made sure their own wishes were carried out. And bureaucrats feel more comfortable with large, identifiable pressure groups or organized institutions than with that intangible unit, the individual. Government departments do not like individuals: those that speak up or are too assertive are troublemakers or irritating 'nut-cases', not worthy of a senior civil servant's attention. Government departments are also, for the same reason, hopeless regulators, as the damning report on the Department of Trade and Industry by an all-party House of Commons committee in 1989 showed.

Even so, ministers must carry some blame for what has happened in Britain. The Government's commitment to increased competition and liberalization went particularly wrong in the case of British Gas, where I believe that in the rush to get as much money as possible for tax cuts prior to an election, ministers decided not to upset the chairman, Sir Denis Rooke, and impose any kind of break-up. There was no need to privatize British Gas whole, and by doing so the Government created a very unpleasant monopoly. To be sure, to have the national gas grid pipeline in one organization is desirable, even necessary, but the supplies of gas should have been opened up to stiff competition both from within Britain and overseas. We must be grateful that the man heading the gas regulatory body has been more vociferous and more determined than most: but for him we should all be worse off. But regulation should surely only be used as a measure of last resort, rather like the policeman in real life. And, as American experience shows, especially in the case of the savings and loans crisis, regulators can often get too close to those they are supposed to be regulating. If the policeman is on too familiar terms with the publican, then the chances are that there will be after-hours drinking. If the regulator of financial services is engaged in the business as well as acting as the policeman, then the tendency will be to gloss over irregularities.

It was not as if the Government was not warned. A Tory MP, Rodney Atkinson, writing in a Bow Group paper, *The Energy Policy Mess*, said competitiveness and efficiency should be paramount, and he was right. Said Atkinson:

The principle purpose of privatization is to ensure that assets are owned by those who have the incentive to seek commercial returns on their use, but who are constrained by competing commercial enterprises and therefore the freedom of customers to take their custom elsewhere.

For privatization to be an effective doctrine there surely has to be true competition. How much better it would be if there were several telephone companies in Britain, each competing to provide services through a common telephone network? Wouldn't air services to and from Britain be better and cheaper if there were rival airlines of equal stature working out of the nation's two busiest airports, Heathrow and Gatwick? Why was the British Airports Authority monster allowed to control Heathrow, Gatwick, Stansted and Manchester? Is a private monopoly controlling water supplies really better than a state one?

Privatization, to be successful, also has not only to be fair, but it has to be seen to be fair. In Britain, it has been neither. As we have seen in almost all the major privatizations, the small shareholder has been penalized to the benefit of the large institution, including those from outside either Britain or the European Community of which the United Kingdom is a member. The City of London has enjoyed special privileges which it has neither deserved nor earned.

Small investors need and deserve special encouragement, for two reasons. First, small investors provide a rich diversity of ownership, preventing total control of businesses by major institutions. Second, if small investors are encouraged then they will save their money rather than spend it on consumption. It is worth pausing to reflect that had Thatcher appealed to the savings instinct, rather than to the greed element – involving short-term capital gains through stagging privatization issues – much British cash might have stayed invested in the sharemarket rather than cashed-up to fuel a retail and property boom with disastrous consequences.

Those who pursued privatization later, such as some of the new governments of Eastern Europe, showed a great deal more common sense. Some set up privatization agencies responsible to parliaments and charged with ensuring a fair distribution of assets. Others provided for open tenders.

There have been some unpleasant side effects of privatization. One of them is that the lists of shareholders of the newly-floated corporations have enabled direct mail companies to put together cheap lists of those who have become shareholders for the first time – and then sold those lists to everyone from credit card companies to insurance and unit trust marketing men.

The upshot is that shareholders in British Gas, British Telecom and the water companies have been bombarded with unwanted junk mail, urging them to sell their investments and to use the money to purchase everything from insurance bonds (normally a poor investment) to timeshares (mostly a disastrous investment). Some have even offered to handle the sale of shares for those deciding to dispose of their meagre holdings, provided they took out a unit trust or insurance investment instead; hardly sensible advice, given the charges now imposed on those entering this form of contract.

Neither the Government nor the City or its regulatory body, the Securities and Investment Board, have done anything at all to stop this unpleasant practice. British Telecom led a campaign to persuade the Department of Trade and Industry to repeal legislation which requires the listing of all shareholders' names on a publicly available list – on the grounds that the information was being used by mail order houses for commercial gain. It was wasting its time. The Conservative Party itself was one of the culprits, using the names of BT shareholders in regional mailings to send out leaflets appealing for funds.

Of course, it would be unwise to introduce secrecy over shareholders' registers, so the BT lobby was bound to fail. But it might be sensible to limit disclosure to those with more than 500 or 1,000 shares, or alternatively to legislate that all those accessing registers must sign a declaration that the information will not be used for marketing by direct mail.

What happens if Labour is returned to office in Britain? Will the privatized corporations be renationalized? I think not. Official Labour policy is to put British Telecom, British Gas, the water companies and the electricity supply industry under what is called 'social ownership' – a euphemism for nationalization. A Labour government would take an unspecified stake in British Aerospace and Rolls-Royce. British Airways and other privatizations would be left alone.

A Labour Party pamphlet, *Social Ownership*, recommends a

socialist government to offer BT shareholders the option of either £1.30 cash – the price at which British Telecom was floated – or a swap for two new government pieces of paper, one an income bond, the other a bond geared to capital growth. Until this happens the government would use its clout in the boardroom, by introducing policies like industrial democracy.

Since the only Labour government likely to be elected is a middle-of-the-road one, I personally believe that potential ministers like John Smith will decide to leave well alone, and get on with other priorities. Party dogma will not benefit the great utilities, or enable them to serve the public interest. But divining new rules so that they behave less like monopolies certainly will. If Labour kept competition in mind, and directed its fire at the City rather than the private investor, it would not run into too much opposition.

Action must be taken to curb monopoly power, regardless of which party is in government. In the case of British Telecom, which has been a disappointment for consumers and business alike, the Government should consider breaking it up into smaller units. OFTEL needs more powers, and it needs to spread its concern beyond the commercial and the economic to those of the telephone user.

It should also allow the many companies who have their own private leased lines between offices or plants in various cities to subsidize their own costs by sub-leasing time on them to outsiders if they wish. If this happened, a company in London could dial into another company's own line to Glasgow, and hence into the Glasgow network, reducing the price of a long-distance call. At present, the Government prohibits this by allowing a restrictive practice.

The Government should also permit companies who have private satellite networks to allow others to use them for common carriage of television pictures or data. At present, the restrictions add to television and radio production costs – and are anti-competitive.

And the politicians must get the pricing and allocation right. While the first big issue – British Telecom – was undoubtedly popular because it was cheap and allowed ordinary members of the public to make a useful capital gain, the family investor has been the loser with more recent issues. The allocations in the cases of British Airways and the British Airports Authority were so small that they were almost useless as a capital gains investment, while the dividends have never been spectacular. By contrast, the City had a field day: the allocations of the institutions were so large they could make big profits by selling on to overseas buyers.

The Government made, I believe, a huge mistake in relying on its friends in the City for pricing advice. I am surprised that Margaret Thatcher fell for it: she, above all, has a keen sense of value.

It would surely be sensible for the British Government – and other governments across the world who are undergoing privatizations – to follow the example of the Japanese with NTT and sell only 10 per cent of the stock initially. This both creates a real demand and provides adequate insurance against making a mistake if the price is seen to be too low. After all, even in the dealing that occurs prior to any large takeover bid, it is unusual for more than 10 per cent of a stock to change hands overnight.

Since Britain is part of the European Community – and since it is only a matter of time before there is political and economic union – it also makes sense to open up all privatizations to Europeans, and not to restrict them. The Thatcher Government has never made more than 20 per cent of a privatization issue available to Europeans – or other overseas investors. Were they to do so the pricing could be more realistic.

Another possibility is to introduce tendering for underwriting, and then offer the shares to the public at a discount to the tender offer. Under such a system, those who wished to be considered as underwriters would tender the premium they would charge for underwriting a privatization, in exactly the same way as someone tendering for a public construction contract.

After all, the great state corporations that have been sold – or are about to be sold by governments – do not belong to the politicians in office, or to the party in government, although ministers, particularly in Britain, have often behaved as if that is the case. They are merely custodians for the period they are in office: the real owners are us, the people. That is why ministers have a duty to get the most for us in any sale. It is the same duty as that of a trustee liquidating a family estate, although the government has two distinct advantages. It can pick its time and does not have to sell when the markets are limp or liquidity is poor. It can also use its publicity machine to stoke up interest.

Of course, it could be argued that the fairest way of disposing of state corporations would be to give them away to the people, or perhaps to the customers. Shares could be allocated in equal proportions to everyone submitting a tax return – on the day they submit it. Individuals would be free to sell their shares at any time thereafter. Under this arrangement, the market would set the price. The Thatcher Government is, after all, supposedly in favour of a market economy. There would then be no question of the Government receiving an artificial boost to the public sector borrowing requirement or receiving a large sum from which it could hand back a proportion as a pre-election tax 'bribe'. There would also be no need for advisers, merchant banks, public relations people or advertising campaigns. £200 million could have been saved on the latter alone.

The principal objection to this arrangement – apart from the fact that it is too simple by half – is that it would not ensure an equal distribution amongst the people. Our children would not benefit. Those with large families would be severely discriminated against. It would also be extremely difficult to cut out non-British people from the issue.

Of course, there is no reason why the system should not be simplified to cut out the middle man. Perhaps the best way of doing this is to value each state body on its present asset value, regardless of estimates of brand value or future earnings prospects. The shares could then be put on sale at value at local post offices or banks, upon production of a National Insurance card. Each card-holder would only be allowed to purchase a certain number; and after the public have had their chance, the unsold could be auctioned to institutions.

One way or another, a better way of privatizing the state needs to be found. For what has happened so far is little more than selling off the family silver.

Index